MEDITATE ON YOUR SPIRITUAL INHERITANCE

Daily Devotions
Explaining Who You Are and
What You Have IN CHRIST

Susan Patricia Schrader

1

❖ACKNOWLEDGEMENTS❖

THANKS TO...

Jesus Christ, for putting this book on my heart and allowing me to be His vessel to work through. For His wisdom and revelation He has given in this book.

My husband, for his love and support while writing this book and for helping me with the final preparation to get it printed.

Christian Photo Shops   www.christianphotoshops.com

Resources:

Amplified Bible, Classic Edition (AMPC). Copyright © 1954, 1958, 1962, 1964, 1965, 1987 by The Lockman Foundation

New Living Translation, (NLT). *Holy Bible,* New Living Translation, copyright © 1996, 2004, 2015 by Tyndale House Foundation.

New Spirit-Filled Life Bible. Copyright 2002, 2013 by Thomas Nelson, Inc. Word-Wealth, Truth in Action, NLT Dictionary

The Passion Translation (TPT). The Passion Translation®. Copyright © 2017 by BroadStreet Publishing® Group, LLC.

Dictionary. Com. 2017 Dictionary.Com, LLC

TABLE OF CONTENTS

❖INTRODUCTION❖

This is my second book in the Meditate on God's Word series. The first one was on prayer. This book will be set up the same way as the first one except the summary will be questions for you to answer to summarize it yourself. The Lord desires for His children to get into the Word more and meditate on it. Meditate means to reflect; to moan, to mutter; to ponder; to make a quiet sound such as sighing; to meditate or contemplate something as one repeats the words.

Reflect and ponder the Scriptures until you have them down in your spirit. It isn't necessarily memorizing the verse but reflecting on it and asking the Lord for the revelation of it. Meditating on the Word is meditating on Jesus because He is the Word made flesh (John 1:1).

You will have success in your life if you meditate on the Word day and night. You must get the Word in your spirit rather than just in your mind if you want to receive insight and revelation from the Lord.

How can a person meditate day and night? The same way we are to pray continually. By being constantly in a state of communion and fellowship with God and reflecting on the Word rather than reading just to be reading. It is good to just read the Word but it is better to take a portion of Scripture and meditate on it until you understand it and receive insight and revelation of it.

In this devotion, I am taking portions of Scripture a week for 52 weeks regarding your spiritual inheritance and meditating on that portion all week. After each day, I give a prayer or declaration on that Scripture. These are to just get you started with your prayers. At the end of the week, I give questions to help you summarize the week. You can go on and study it further or go on to the next week's portion of Scripture. I recommend you only do the daily devotion which is short and reflect and meditate on it rather than complete the whole week in one day.

It is important to get into a routine of meditating on the Word of God. I only gave the reference of the verses I'm using because you need to look up these verses and read them from your Bible rather than just reading them from this book. I may not talk about the whole portion of Scripture I have given but it is important to read the whole context around it.

I have written these devotions from Jesus' point of view; i.e., the first person singular (I, Me, Mine) always refers to Christ or Father God. "You" refers to you, the reader, so the idea is that of Jesus speaking to you.

An inheritance is an acquisition of a possession, condition, or trait from past generations; something that is or may be inherited. Inherited is to take possession as a rightful heir. Usually you inherit something when a family member or loved one passes on.

Most Christians think they will have eternal life after they pass on and receive everything else promised in the Word after they pass on. They think the only benefit they have as a Christian is forgiveness of their sins and their name written in the Book of Life and a home in heaven in the sweet by and by. This is not the case.

We have an inheritance and we don't have to die to get it. Jesus has already died to get it for us. Jesus bore the curse of the law so that the blessings could come upon you and me.

Ephesians 1:11 New Living Translation (NLT) Furthermore, because we are united with Christ, we have received an inheritance from God, for he chose us in advance, and he makes everything work out according to his plan.

This verse says we have received an inheritance from God because we are united with Christ. It is NOW not in the future.

Colossians 1:12 New Living Translation (NLT) Always thanking the Father. He has enabled you to share in the inheritance that belongs to his people, who live in the light.

This inheritance from God belongs to us as soon as we accept Jesus as our Lord and Savior. The reason for this book is to help you realize this inheritance belongs to you and who you are and what you have IN CHRIST. Your identity is in Him.

WEEK 1
❖MADE ALIVE WITH CHRIST❖

❖DAY 1❖
Read Ephesians 2

Before you accepted Me as your Lord and Savior, you were dead and separated from Father God because of your sins. You were born in sin because of the disobedience of Adam and Eve in the garden. Father God told them not to eat of the tree of knowledge of good and evil. They listened to the serpent and they immediately were spiritually dead and separated from our Father God. They didn't die physically right away but they were spiritually dead immediately.

When you were physically born, you were born of Adam and of sin. That is why Father God sent Me to die on the cross so that you may become spiritually alive and no longer separated from Father God.

Father, thank You for sending Jesus to take my sins so I no longer am separated from You. In Jesus' name Amen.

❖DAY 2❖
Read Ephesians 2

You were, by nature, children of Father God's wrath before you accepted Me as your Lord and Savior. Our Father God was so rich in mercy because of His great and wonderful love for you even when you were separated from Him because of your sins. He made you spiritually alive together with Me by His grace and saved you from His judgment.

Father, thank You for making me alive in Christ and saving me from Your judgment. In Jesus' name Amen.

❖ DAY 3 ❖
Read Ephesians 2

What is grace? It is our undeserved favor and mercy. Also, it is our remarkable compassion and favor. I (Jesus) am "grace".

This salvation is not through your own effort but it is My gracious gift to you. It is not as a result of your works so no one can take credit. It is only through Me that you can be saved. Father loved you so much that He sent Me to die for you. I came willingly because of My love and the Father's love.

Father, thank You for Your grace, Your mercy and Your love for me and for sending Jesus to die for me. It is only through faith in Jesus that I am saved from Your judgment. In Jesus' name Amen.

❖ DAY 4 ❖
Read Ephesians 2

You are a work of art, created in Me. You are spiritually transformed and renewed to do good things I have planned for you. By My blood shed on the cross, you have access to the throne of Father God. You are no longer separated from Him.

We love you so much and desire communion with you. Come boldly to the throne and through Me you can speak freely to our Father (Hebrews 4:16).

Father, thank You for transforming me and renewing me and allowing me to boldly come into Your presence. I declare I am a masterpiece You have created. In Jesus' name Amen.

❖DAY 5❖
Read Ephesians 2

You are raised from the dead along with Me and seated with Me in the heavenly realm, which is the invisible realm that surrounds you not the home you are destined for, because you are united with Me.

I have given you every spiritual blessing that belongs to Me in the heavenly realm because you are united with Me. These blessings are yours NOW not when you die because you are "in Me" NOW.

Father, I declare I am seated in the heavenly realm and have been given every spiritual blessing because I am united in Christ. In Jesus' name Amen.

❖DAY 6❖
Read Ephesians 2

In Me you are now a member of Father God's family, a joint heir with Me (Romans 8:17). You became one spirit with Me. Father God sees you in Me. You are a child of God, just as I am His Son. You are My holy temple that My Spirit dwells in (1 Corinthians 3:16).

You need to see yourself in Me and know the reality of it and all the blessings you have in Me.

Thank You, Father, for adopting me into Your family and being a joint heir with Jesus. I declare I am Your child and have all the blessings that Jesus has. In Jesus' name Amen.

Read Ephesians 2

1. Why were you separated from Father God before you accepted Me as your Lord and Savior?

2. What made you spiritually alive together with Me?

3. What is grace? Is salvation from your own efforts and works?

4. By My blood shed on the cross, what access do you now have?

5. Where are you now seated and with who?

6. Who are you a joint-heir with? What do you receive by being in the family of God? When do you receive these things?

NOTES:

WEEK 2
❖A NEW CREATURE❖
ตตตตตตตตตตตต

❖DAY 1❖
Read 2 Corinthians 5:17-21

If you accepted Me, Jesus Christ, as your Lord and Savior, you are a new creation. You were hoping by this verse that everything would be different in your mind and body, as well as your spirit. The only thing that is brand new is your spirit. Your mind and body have to be renewed by My Word to be changed and transformed.

You can be transformed completely by the renewing of your mind by My Word (Romans 12:2). Once you understand who you are in Me and what you have in Me, you will be transformed.

Thank You, Father, for sending Jesus to die for me so that I can be a new creation in Christ. I am renewing my mind to Your Word so that I can be transformed to Your ways. In Jesus' name Amen.

❖DAY 2❖
Read 2 Corinthians 5:17-21

Your spirit is brand new. You were living in sin and separated from our Father God before you accepted Me. I came and took your sin and sicknesses and set you free from sin and bondage. I gave My life willingly so that you could come boldly into our Father God's presence and commune with Him. Our Father God loved you so much that He sent Me to die for your sins. I took all your sin upon the cross and you are no longer a slave to sin. You are forgiven of all sin.

Through the shedding of My blood, you are now a child of our Father God (Ephesians 1:5) and a joint heir with Me. You have inherited all the blessings that I have (Ephesians 1:11). You have everything you need for life and godliness (2 Peter 1:3).

Father, I declare I can come boldly into Your presence and commune with You. Thank You for forgiving me of all my sins and giving me every spiritual blessing and all I need for life and godliness in Christ. I am Your child and a joint heir with Jesus. In Jesus' name Amen.

❖DAY 3❖
Read 2 Corinthians 5:17-21

I want you to know what the fresh and new is. Your spirit has been created brand new. You have been created in My image. In your spirit, you are a "new species of being that never existed before". When you accepted Me as Lord and Savior, you were brought into existence by My creative power. The old has passed away, the fresh and new has come.

There are many, many things I have given to you. There are many promises in My Word that you can claim. Many are conditional to your obedience to My Word and spiritual laws.

This new life is a gift to be reconciled to our Father God through Me. You are righteous in My sight through My blood shed on the cross (2 Corinthians 5:21). Our Father only sees My blood that took your sin. You can boldly come into My presence. Don't be sin conscious anymore thinking of your unworthiness. You are worthy through My blood. I have forgiven you of all your sin. Come believing and confessing that you are righteous in My sight. You are in right standing with Me if you are born again. You are no longer a slave to sin but a slave to righteousness.

Father, I declare I am righteous before You. I am in right standing with You. I will come boldly into Your presence and commune with You. I love You Lord. In Jesus' name Amen.

❖DAY 4❖
Read 2 Corinthians 5:17-21

You are My ambassador or representative to reconcile others to Me. I send you out to boldly proclaim My love and to tell others to come back to Me.

I will lead you and direct your steps to those who need to hear about Father God reconciling all men to Him through Me.

Father, I declare I am Your ambassador. I belong to You as Your beloved child. I allow You to lead and guide me in all things. I commune with You and enjoy Your presence. In Jesus' name Amen.

❖DAY 5❖
Read 2 Corinthians 5:17-21

You can do all things through Me because I empower you with strength (Philippians 4:13). You are not weak but strong. The Spirit that raised Me from the dead dwells in you so you have power and strength to do all that I called you to.

My healing power dwells in you. By My stripes you were healed (1 Peter 2:24). Healing was provided on the cross. Through Me I forgave you all your sins and healed all your diseases (Psalm 103:3).

You must believe when you pray and you will receive. Healing is in your spirit, you need to learn how to release it in the natural. Just as you must have faith to receive salvation, you have to have faith for healing to manifest. Don't be moved by what you see or feel, be moved only by what My Word says and you will receive.

Father, I declare I can do all things through Christ who empowers me. Thank You for Your healing power that dwells in me. I believe and I receive what You have provided. In Jesus' name Amen.

❖DAY 6❖
Read 2 Corinthians 5:17-21

You are more than a conqueror through Me and have the victory in this life (Romans 8:37). You may not feel victorious but you are. I have given you all authority and power to overcome all attacks of Satan. You have it all dwelling in you. It's up to you to release it. I will back you up but I've sent you to heal the sick and set the captives free. Don't say "God get the devil off of me". I've told you to resist the devil and he will flee.

You are My representative on the earth and I've given you all you need to do what I've called you to do. I'm waiting on you to get that revelation and move in My power and authority.

Father, I declare I am more than a conqueror through Christ and have the victory through the power and authority that has been given to me. I am to go and heal the sick and set the captives free as Your representative on this earth. I will walk in the power and authority You have given to me. In Jesus' name Amen.

❖ DAY 7 - SUMMARY ❖
Read 2 Corinthians 5:17-21

1. When you accepted Jesus as your Lord and Savior you became a new creation. Was your body and mind renewed or just your spirit?

2. What are you a slave to now that you are in Christ?

3. How does God see you after accepting Jesus?

4. How many sins were forgiven through Jesus' blood shed on the cross? How many diseases were healed?

5. Where are all these promises from the Word dwelling?

6. How do you release these promises?

NOTES:

WEEK 3
❖LIFE IN THE SPIRIT❖

❖DAY 1❖
Read Romans 8:1-17; Ephesians 1:13-14

There is no condemnation for those who are in Me and walk after the Spirit. I have redeemed you from sin and death.

What does no condemnation mean? It means that if you are in Me, then you are no longer guilty because of sin. I took all your sins away. They were placed on Me so that you would not be judged or condemned of any wrong. There is no judgment against anyone who believes in Me (John 3:18).

Thank You, Father, for sending Jesus so that I am not condemned or judged for my sins or any wrong because Jesus took them all away, my sins were placed on Jesus. In Jesus' name Amen.

❖DAY 2❖
Read Romans 8:1-17; Ephesians 1:13-14

Because you belong to Me, the power of My life giving Spirit has freed you from the power of sin and death. I know you wonder why you still struggle with sin. You must acknowledge My Spirit that is in you and follow after My Spirit and be led by My Spirit not your flesh or your carnal mind. I sent My Holy Spirit to be your helper, intercessor, comforter, advocate and counselor. My Holy Spirit is available to you, dwells in you and provides all these things. You are sealed by My Holy Spirit as My possession.

The only way to overcome sin is to feed your spirit with My Word so that your spirit becomes stronger than your flesh. You need to renew your mind to My Word.

Father, I declare I will feed my spirit with Your Word so that my spirit becomes stronger than my flesh. I will renew my mind to Your Word. In Jesus' name Amen.

❖DAY 3❖
Read Romans 8:1-17; Ephesians 1:13-14

My Spirit dwells within you (1 Corinthians 3:16). By My Spirit dwelling in you, you should be controlled by My Spirit. If you are dominated by the sinful nature you will think about sinful things. You cannot please Me if you are dominated by the sinful nature.

If you are controlled by your sinful nature it will lead to death. Those who do not have My Spirit living in them do not belong to Me.

If you let the Spirit control your mind, it will lead to life and peace. You are controlled by My Spirit if you have My Spirit living in you. I do live in you and give you life.

Father, I declare that Your Spirit dwells within me and I am controlled by Your Spirit and I have life and peace. In Jesus' name Amen.

❖DAY 4❖
Read Romans 8:1-17; Ephesians 1:13-14

The same Spirit that raised Me from the dead dwells within you. Think about that for a minute. Think about the power of the Spirit that is available to you through Me. Abba both raised Me up and also will raise you up by that power that dwells within you.

If you are led by My Spirit, you are sons of God. This describes the lifestyle of those who are sons of God. This means to progressively put to death the sinful appetites of the lower nature.

All Christians are generally being led by My Spirit but there are increasing degrees of being led by My Spirit. The more fully you are led by My Spirit, the more completely you will be obedient to Me and be conformed to My standards. Being led by My Spirit is a process, it is continual not a one-time experience.

Father, I declare Your powerful Spirit dwells in me and will raise me up and lead me to be obedient and conformed to You. In Jesus' name Amen.

❖DAY 5❖
Read Romans 8:1-17; Ephesians 1:13-14

You have not received a spirit of bondage to fear but a spirit of adoption. You can call God, Abba daddy. You have been adopted into our family. You are a joint heir with Me and Abba daddy is your father. He loves you as much as He loves Me.

I love you as much as He loves you. That is why I agreed to come to die for you so you could be adopted into the family. He wants you to freely come to Him and call Him Abba daddy. Through My shed blood on the cross you can do that freely and boldly. My Spirit bears witness with your spirit that you are children of Abba daddy.

Father, I declare I am adopted into Your family and can boldly come into Your presence and call You Abba daddy through the shed blood of Jesus. Thank You, Jesus. In Jesus' name Amen.

❖DAY 6❖
Read Romans 8:1-17; Ephesians 1:13-14

You shall be glorified with Me just as you will share in My suffering. You will have trials and tribulations in this world but I have overcome the world.

You have been redeemed from sickness and poverty but you have not been redeemed from persecution. If you are a Christian, you will be persecuted for your faith. Maybe some worse than others depending on what I have called you to. I will comfort you through your suffering so that you can comfort others that are suffering (2 Corinthians 1:4).

Father, I thank You for sending Jesus to redeem me from sickness and poverty. I know I may be persecuted for my faith in Jesus but I will not fear. You will comfort me through my suffering so I can comfort others. I will trust in You and be led by the Holy Spirit. In Jesus' name Amen.

19

Read Romans 8:1-17; Ephesians 1:13-14

1. What does condemnation mean?

2. What has the life giving Spirit freed you from?

3. Where does the Spirit of God dwell?

4. Are you being led by the Spirit of God?

5. What kind of spirit have you received? What can you call God? Who are you a joint heir with?

6. What kind of suffering will you experience?

NOTES:

WEEK 4
❖GIFT OF RIGHTEOUSNESS❖

❖DAY 1❖
Read Romans 3:21-26; 2 Corinthians 5:21
Ephesians 6:14

You are made right by placing your faith in Me. No matter who you are, it is by faith in Me. You are righteous, in right standing because of My blood shed on the cross. I took your sin and made you righteous.

I freed you from the penalty of your sins because I was the sacrifice on the cross for your sins. Believe that I was the sacrifice for your sins and you are made righteous in Abba's eyes.

Father, thank You for Jesus being my sacrifice for my sins and making me righteous in Your eyes. In Jesus' name Amen.

❖DAY 2❖
Read Romans 3:21-26; 2 Corinthians 5:21
Ephesians 6:14

Abba's judgment and wrath was fully put upon Me, the blameless sacrifice, for all sins both past and present. It is faith in My blood that you are justified in Abba's eyes. Justified means you can say "just as if I never sinned". In Abba's eyes, you have never sinned and are totally righteous in Him.

Father, I declare I have faith in the shed blood of Jesus and I am justified in Your eyes. I am righteous before You. In Jesus' name Amen.

❖DAY 3❖
Read Romans 3:21-26; 2 Corinthians 5:21
Ephesians 6:14

Righteousness means in right standing with Me. It is conformity to My revealed will in all respects. I declare you righteous (Romans 3:24). I have made you right and also have made you pure, holy, and free from sin (1 Corinthians 1:30).

Righteousness is only by faith. It is a gift. Nothing you do will make you righteous but it refers to uprightness in character and conduct.

Father, I declare I am righteous before You because You declare me righteous, in right standing with You and pure and holy in Your sight through the blood of Jesus. In Jesus' name Amen.

❖DAY 4❖
Read Romans 3:21-26; 2 Corinthians 5:21
Ephesians 6:14

I have also provided you with Abba's armor that you are to put on. I don't put it on you but I do provide it. You have to put it on yourself! Within this armor is the breastplate of righteousness with the belt of truth holding it.

This is My righteousness that I have given you and as a breastplate it protects you from the neck to the upper part of your thighs, your entire trunk and vital organs. The spiritual battle is integrity (character) and righteous living (conduct) because these qualities are mine and the new creation I bring to you. Lack of integrity will expose you to the enemy.

Father, I declare I have the breastplate of righteousness on and walk in integrity and righteousness. I walk in the qualities of Jesus. In Jesus' name Amen.

Read Romans 3:21-26; 2 Corinthians 5:21
Ephesians 6:14

You need to be righteousness conscious rather than sin conscious in your walk with Me. Even when you sin and fail, you are righteous in My eyes. You are worthy because of My shed blood on the cross.

Developing a righteousness consciousness will cause you to live an overcoming, victorious life. Abba wants to treat you as if you had never sinned. He sent Me to the cross to bear your sin, to completely wash away the sin that had been in you. Because you are in Me, Abba sees you the same way He sees Me. He wants to treat you like He treats Me. You are worthy of Our love.

Father, I declare I am righteousness conscious rather than sin conscious and live an overcoming, victorious life because of Jesus washing away all my sin. Thank You. In Jesus' name Amen.

❖DAY 6❖
Read Romans 3:21-26; 2 Corinthians 5:21
Ephesians 6:14

By My overflowing grace and the free gift of righteousness, you are a royal priesthood, chosen and accepted into the family, you reign as kings in this life through Me.

How does a king live in this life? He pretty much has everything he wants and needs. You also reign in this life as kings and have everything you need for life and godliness. You reign over sickness and disease. You reign over poverty and every kind of evil.

Father, I declare I have Your overflowing grace and the gift of righteousness and reign as a king in this life. I have all that I need from You for life and godliness. In Jesus' name Amen.

❖DAY 7 – SUMMARY QUESTIONS❖
Read Romans 3:21-26; 2 Corinthians 5:21
Ephesians 6:14

1. How are you made right in God's eyes?

2. What does justified mean?

3. What does righteousness mean? What makes us righteous?

4. What has Jesus provided us with?

5. What kind of consciousness does God want you to develop to be victorious in life?

6. What does Jesus' grace and free gift of righteousness cause you to be?

NOTES:

WEEK 5
❖LIVE AND MOVE AND EXIST IN HIM❖
❧❧❧❧❧❧❧❧❧❧❧❧❧❧❧❧❧❧❧❧

❖DAY 1❖
Read Acts 17:28; Colossians 1:17
John 15:1-8

In Me you live and move and exist. You are made alive in Me (Ephesians 2:1, 5). Before you accepted Me, you were dead in your trespasses and sins but when you accepted Me as your Lord and Savior, you were made alive in Me. Your identity is in Me.

You live in Me as a branch is made alive by the vine. You must maintain an abiding union with Me to stay alive and bear fruit.

Father, I declare I live and move and have my being in You. You made me alive when I accepted You as Lord and Savior. I will maintain an abiding union with You to stay alive and bear fruit. In Jesus' name Amen.

❖DAY 2❖
Read Acts 17:28; Colossians 1:17
John 15:1-8

I am the vine, you are the branches. You abide in Me and I in you and you will bear much fruit. I know you wonder how you can abide in Me?

You abide in Me by accepting Me as your Lord and Savior and getting My Word into your spirit. I abide in you by My Holy Spirit dwelling in you. You can do nothing without abiding in Me; just as the branch cannot bear fruit without being attached to the vine.

You must be dependent on Me and acknowledge Me in all things.

Father, I declare I abide in You and You abide in me. I stay completely connected to You as the branch stays connected to the vine to be able to bear fruit. In Jesus' name Amen.

❖DAY 3❖
Read Acts 17:28; Colossians 1:17
John 15:1-8

I am before all things and in Me all things exist and are held together. Just as the branch is attached to the vine, you are connected to Me and held together only through Me.

I give you life just as the vine gives the branch life. If the branch becomes disconnected, it will not bear fruit and will wither away. If a branch is snapped partly from the vine, it will eventually die and be thrown away. It needs to be completely attached and connected. If not, it won't get all the life and nourishment that is needed to stay alive and bear fruit. It is the same with Me, you must stay completely attached and connected to Me to stay alive and bear fruit.

Father, I declare I am held together, attached and connected completely to You as the branch is connected to the vine to give life and bear fruit. In Jesus' name Amen.

❖DAY 4❖
Read Acts 17:28; Colossians 1:17
John 15:1-8

You must abide in Me and My Word must abide in you. I am the Word of life. My Spirit dwells in you and gives you life and helps you bear fruit. Be led by My Spirit and stay connected to the written Word given to you.

My Words will give you life, show you how to bear the fruit provided, and show you things to come and how to be an overcomer. It must remain in you. The only way for it to remain or abide in you is by you reading and meditating on it continuously.

Father, I declare I abide in You and Your Word abides in me. I will bear much fruit and be an overcomer because I meditate on Your Word and stay connected to the Word. In Jesus' name Amen.

❖DAY 5❖
Read Acts 17:28; Colossians 1:17
John 15:1-8

I know you wonder what this fruit is that you will bear. Answered prayer is one fruit you will bear to glorify our Father. You can ask what you desire and it will be given to you. I and My Word must abide in you to have your prayers answered.

When I and My Word abide in you, your desires will be My desires and you ask what you desire and it will be given to you. Delight yourself in Me and I will give you the desires of your heart (Psalm 37:4).

Father, I declare as I delight in You and Your Word abides in me, You will give me the desires of my heart. My desires will glorify You. In Jesus' name Amen.

❖DAY 6❖
Read Acts 17:28; Colossians 1:17
John 15:1-8

Other fruit that you will bear if I and My Word are abiding in you is the fruit of My Spirit which is love, joy, peace, patience, kindness, goodness, faithfulness, gentleness and self-control (Galatians 5:22-23).

All of this fruit dwells within you because My Spirit dwells within you. As you read My Word and renew your mind, you will grow in this fruit. It is available to you. You just need to realize it is there for you and tap into it to manifest in your life.

Father, I declare I will bear the fruit of the Spirit in my life which is love, joy, peace, patience, kindness, goodness, faithfulness, gentleness and self-control. In Jesus' name Amen.

❖DAY 7 – SUMMARY QUESTIONS❖
Read Acts 17:28; Colossians 1:17
John 15:1-8

1. How do you live in Christ?

2. How do you abide in Christ?

3. How are you connected and held together in Christ?

4. What is the fruit you will bear by being connected to Christ?

5. Where is this fruit?

6. How will you grow in this fruit?

NOTES:

WEEK 6
❖LOVE❖

❖DAY 1❖
Read Galatians 5:16-26; I Corinthians 13:4-8

The fruit you will bear by being connected to Me is the fruit of My Spirit. This fruit is My character and conduct and it dwells within you because My Holy Spirit dwells within you.

There are nine characteristics of this fruit which is love, joy, peace, patience, kindness, goodness, faithfulness, gentleness, and self-control. The first three concern your attitude to Me, the second three deals with social relationships, and the last three describes principles that guide a Christian's conduct.

Father, I am connected to You as the branch is connected to the vine and I will bear fruit which is the fruit of the Spirit. I will walk in love because You are love and I know You and I am Your child. You are love and Your Spirit dwells in me. In Jesus' name Amen.

❖DAY 2❖
Read Galatians 5:16-26; I Corinthians 13:4-8

I am love (I John 4:8) and anyone who does not love does not know Me. If you know Me and are a child of God then you will love one another. My love is the foundation to all the fruit. Without My love, the other characteristics of My fruit will not manifest.

I know you are thinking there are some people that are just unlovable and impossible for you to even think about loving but I am love. My Spirit dwells in you and will help you to love that unlovable person.

Allow My love to flow from your spirit to that unlovable person. It is a sacrifice because you have to die to your flesh to allow My love to flow from you.

Father, I do have problems loving some people but Your Spirit and Your love dwells in me and I will allow Your love to flow out of me to love the unlovable. In Jesus' name Amen.

29

❖DAY 3❖
Read Galatians 5:16-26; I Corinthians 13:4-8

My love is patient and kind. My love is not jealous or boastful or proud or rude. My love does not demand its own way. It is not irritable and it keeps no record of being wronged. My love does not rejoice about injustice but rejoices whenever the truth wins out.

My love never gives up, never loses faith, is always hopeful and endures through every circumstance. My love will last forever! My love is unconditional. Nothing you do will change My love for you.

You have this love dwelling within you. My Spirit dwells within you desiring to help you manifest this love.

Father, I declare Your love dwells within me and with the Holy Spirit helping me, I can walk in this love and it will manifest in my life. In Jesus' name Amen.

❖DAY 4❖
Read Galatians 5:16-26; I Corinthians 13:4-8

First, My love is patient which covers a multitude of sins. If you see someone who is in sin do not blab it to everyone. Protect them from others as you speak to your leaders or confront them in love. You have all sinned and come short of My glory, so do not judge.

Do not be boastful or proud thinking you are better than others. You are to think of others better than yourself and be helpful to them, (Philippians 2:4) and do not be rude. Don't be concerned for your own good but for the good of others (1 Corinthians 10:24).

My love does not demand its own way. You are not to demand your own way, but listen to the other person and discuss in love for an agreeable answer.

Father, I will be patient and cover up the sins of others. I will protect them in love. I will not judge. I will not be boastful or proud but think of others better than myself. I will not demand my own way. In Jesus' name Amen.

❖DAY 5❖
Read Galatians 5:16-26; I Corinthians 13:4-8

I know you are keeping a record of wrongdoing done to you from certain people. My love does not keep a record of wrongdoing nor is it irritable.

You have My love dwelling in you that will help you to walk in love and forgiveness. You are not to be irritable and annoyed by others. Allow My love to flow through you to that annoying person. Forgive them and wipe the slate clean. Keeping a record of their wrongdoing only causes more irritation.

Father, I declare I will not keep a record of wrongdoing nor allow them to irritate me. I will walk in love and forgiveness and wipe the slate clean with Your help Lord. In Jesus' name Amen.

❖DAY 6❖
Read Galatians 5:16-26; I Corinthians 13:4-8

My love never gives up. My love never loses faith. It is always hopeful and endures through every circumstance. My love dwells in you because My Spirit dwells in you. I AM love. Nothing is impossible to you as long as you stay focused on Me and on My Word.

I love you so very much and want you to experience My love and allow it to manifest in your life so you can love others. It is possible to love the unlovable and walk in forgiveness. When you get the revelation of My love, you will be able to walk in My love.

Father, I declare I will walk in Your love. I will never give up. I will never lose faith. I will always be hopeful and endure through every circumstance because Your love dwells in me and is manifested in my life. In Jesus' name Amen.

❖DAY 7 – SUMMARY QUESTIONS❖
Read Galatians 5:16-26; I Corinthians 13:4-8

1. What is the fruit of the Spirit in relation to Jesus? Where is this fruit?

2. What is the foundation of the fruit of the Spirit?

3. God is….?

4. Describe the love of God?

5. Where does the love of God dwell?

6. Is it possible to love the unlovable and walk in forgiveness?

NOTES:

WEEK 7
❖JOY❖

❖DAY 1❖
Read Galatians 5:16-26
Nehemiah 8:1-10; Zephaniah 3:17

Joy is a fruit of My Spirit. My joy will give you strength. Joy is part of My character. I rejoice over you with singing. I leap for joy and spin around with intense motion over you because of My love for you.

My joy isn't just a quiet, inner sense of well-being. I dance over you and get excited over you. This joy is within you because My Spirit is within you. Be joyful in all things.

Father, I declare I have the fruit of joy in my life and this joy gives me strength. I will be joyful in all things. In Jesus' name Amen.

❖DAY 2❖
Read Galatians 5:16-26
Nehemiah 8:1-10; Zephaniah 3:17

How does My joy give you strength? A happy heart is good medicine and a joyful mind causes healing. But a broken spirit dries up the bones and zaps your strength (Proverbs 17:22 AMP).

My joy is healing to your mind and body. When your spirit is broken it zaps your strength. Even in the midst of trials, My joy will strengthen you and heal you.

Thank You, Father, for the joy that is in my heart and strengthens me and heals me. In Jesus' name Amen.

❖DAY 3❖
Read Galatians 5:16-26
Nehemiah 8:1-10; Zephaniah 3:17

I know you are wondering how a person can be joyful with all that is going on in this world. My joy is not the same as happiness. Happiness comes from the outside. It is a fleeting, temporal condition that depends on the comfort of your flesh. My joy comes from the inside. It is based on the condition of your heart. When you get a revelation of My joy that is within you, you will be able to be joyful no matter what is going on around you.

My presence is always with you, so My joy is always with you. When trials come focus on Me and My Word and My joy will strengthen you.

Father, I declare that no matter what is going on around me, I will focus on You and Your Word and allow Your joy to be released from my spirit so that I can stay strong even in the midst of trials. In Jesus' name Amen.

❖DAY 4❖
Read Galatians 5:16-26
Nehemiah 8:1-10; Zephaniah 3:17

Remember Paul and Silas when they were in prison (Acts 16:24-26). They were in stocks in the inner prison but they were joyful in the midst of their trial and praised Me. As they were praising Me, I got so excited from their praises that I started dancing and singing so much that the foundations of the prison were shaken and all the doors were opened and the shackles on all the prisoners were loosed.

Are you in a trial right now? Start praising Me and you will receive the victory. Praise will stir up the joy that is in you.

Father, I declare even in the midst of trials and tribulations, I will praise You and be joyful in the midst of the trials. I will receive the victory. In Jesus' name Amen.

❖DAY 5❖
Read Galatians 5:16-26
Nehemiah 8:1-10; Zephaniah 3:17

How can you stir up My joy? As mentioned already, praise is one way to stir up My joy. I know that when you are in a trial, you don't usually feel joy. Joy is not a feeling; it is a spiritual force, a fruit of My Spirit that dwells in you. Keep praising Me and it will come.

Another way to stir up My joy is by meditating on My Word (Proverbs 4:20-23; Joshua 1:8). When you meditate on My Word revelation will begin to rise up in your heart and joy comes. Get excited and meditate on My Word with expectancy. You'll be surprised of the joy that fills your heart.

Father, I will stir up the joy that is in my heart by praising You and meditating on Your Word. Thank You, Lord, for Your joy. In Jesus' name Amen.

❖DAY 6❖
Read Galatians 5:16-26
Nehemiah 8:1-10; Zephaniah 3:17

Rejoicing is an act of your will (Psalm 27:6; Philippians 4:4). When you don't feel like rejoicing, set your will and rejoice anyway. Keep on rejoicing until you have the victory and you know that you are walking in My joy no matter what is going on.

People will see the joy in your life and come to you asking you how they can get this joy in their lives. You will be able to tell them how to get My joy and maintain it in every trial and be strengthened by it.

Father, I declare I will rejoice in You whether I feel like it or not. I will keep rejoicing until I have the victory. I will know I am walking in Your joy and others will see it and come asking me how to get it. I will be able to tell them. In Jesus' name Amen.

35

Read Galatians 5:16-26
Nehemiah 8:1-10; Zephaniah 3:17

1. What will the joy of the Lord give you?

2. How does joy give you strength?

3. Where is this joy and what is it based on?

4. What did Paul and Silas do and what happened?

5. How can you stir up this joy?

6. Rejoicing is an act of what?

NOTES:

WEEK 8
❖PEACE❖
❧❧❧❧❧❧

❖DAY 1❖
Read Galatians 5:16-26; Philippians 4:6-7
Isaiah 26:3; John 14:27

Peace is a fruit of My Spirit that dwells within you. You are not to worry about anything. Worry will steal your peace. You are to pray about everything.

Talk to Me about your worries and fears. I am always listening to My children and as you thank Me for all that I have done, you will then experience My peace.

Father, I declare I will not worry or fear but pray about everything. I will tell You about all my needs and give You thanks for all You have done, then I will experience Your peace. In Jesus' name Amen.

❖DAY 2❖
Read Galatians 5:16-26; Philippians 4:6-7
Isaiah 26:3; John 14:27

The peace I leave with you is perfect; it is not of this world. It is not the same as natural peace that may be going on in the world. It will reassure your heart. It's beyond your understanding but it will stand guard over your heart and your mind.

Don't let your heart be troubled or afraid. Let My peace calm you in every circumstance and give you courage and strength in every challenge.

Thank You, Father, for leaving me Your peace. It is beyond my understanding but I will not let my heart be troubled. I will trust in You and in Your peace. In Jesus' name Amen.

❖DAY 3❖
Read Galatians 5:16-26; Philippians 4:6-7
Isaiah 26:3; John 14:27

My peace is a state of rest, quietness, and calmness. My peace is absence of strife. It is a state of being unruffled no matter what is going on in your life. It is having a perfect well-being.

I know you find it hard to think you can experience this in your life but you can because My Spirit dwells within you and My peace dwells within you. You need to learn how to tap into it and release it into your life. My Spirit will help you. Meditate on My Word about My peace and confess it into your life.

Father, I declare I will walk in Your peace which is a state of rest, quietness, and calmness. I will not be in strife but be a peace maker. I will be unruffled no matter what comes my way. In Jesus' name Amen.

❖DAY 4❖
Read Galatians 5:16-26; Philippians 4:6-7
Isaiah 26:3; John 14:27

You are to remain in the Secret Place, My presence, and you will have My peace. The main way to remain in the Secret Place is to crucify your flesh because your flesh is what causes you to wander from the Secret Place.

My Word is the only way to crucify your flesh; stay in My Word. Meditate on it day and night and you will find My peace.

Father, I declare I will remain in the Secret Place which is Your presence. I will crucify my flesh by meditating on Your Word and will find Your peace. In Jesus' name Amen.

❖DAY 5❖
Read Galatians 5:16-26; Philippians 4:6-7
Isaiah 26:3; John 14:27

Your mind must stay on Me and My Word and you will have My perfect peace. My perfect peace is health, happiness, and well-being. When your thoughts get onto worldly things, it causes you to wander from the Secret Place, from My presence and My peace. All My fruit are conditional to remaining in Me. It cannot grow without nurturing it.

Just like a seed planted, without it being nurtured and watered, it will not grow. Nurture peace by the water of My Word and it will grow and you will experience My presence, My peace and all My fruit.

Father, I declare I will keep my mind on You and Your Word and I will have Your perfect peace which is health, happiness, and well-being. I will nurture peace by the water of Your Word and experience Your presence and peace. In Jesus' name Amen.

❖DAY 6❖
Read Galatians 5:16-26; Philippians 4:6-7
Isaiah 26:3; John 14:27

Trust in Me with all your heart and lean not on your own understanding (Proverbs 3:5). Trusting Me means you make Me your refuge, your fortress. When you find refuge in Me, you will experience My peace.

Don't lean on your own understanding about anything. I will direct your path if you acknowledge Me in all things (Proverbs 3:6). Remember, My peace passes all understanding. You cannot understand the peace that I give you but you will experience it if you trust in Me. You can only survive in this world by being in My presence.

Father, I declare I will trust You and not lean on my own understanding. I will make You my refuge and fortress and I will have Your peace that passes all understanding. I will not try to understand it but will trust You and experience Your peace. In Jesus' name Amen.

❖DAY 7 – SUMMARY QUESTIONS❖
Read Galatians 5:16-26; Philippians 4:6-7
Isaiah 26:3; John 14:27

1. Where does peace dwell and what can steal it?

2. What will this peace do?

3. What is this peace?

4. What is the Secret Place and how do you stay in it?

5. How do you nurture peace?

6. What does trusting the Lord mean?

NOTES:

WEEK 9
❖PATIENCE❖
ও৶ও৶ও৶ও৶ও৶

❖DAY 1❖
Read Galatians 5:16-26; Hebrews 6:12; Hebrews 10:36
Romans 5:1-5; 1Timothy 6:11; John 16:33

Patience or longsuffering is another fruit of My Spirit. Patience is a constancy of bearing up, holding out, enduring. It is the capacity to bear up in difficult circumstances with a hopeful fortitude that resists weariness and defeat. Constancy is being the same in difficult situations as you are in good situations. It's not the ability to wait, but how you act while waiting.

You can be joyful in these times of troubles knowing that the victory is yours and I am with you through them all.

Father, I declare I walk in the fruit of the Spirit which is patience. I will endure in joy every situation that comes my way. In Jesus' name Amen.

❖DAY 2❖
Read Galatians 5:16-26; Hebrews 6:12; Hebrews 10:36
Romans 5:1-5; 1Timothy 6:11; John 16:33

You are to pursue true riches which are spiritual riches such as righteousness, godliness, faith, love, patience, and gentleness. Patience dwells within you but you must pursue it, grow and mature in it. It will not happen without you studying and meditating on my Word and pursuing it.

Father, I declare I will pursue true spiritual riches which are righteousness, godliness, faith, love, patience and gentleness. I will study Your Word and grow in patience. In Jesus' name Amen.

❖DAY 3❖
Read Galatians 5:22-23; Hebrews 6:12; Hebrews 10:36
Romans 5:1-5; 1Timothy 6:11; John 16:33

Be humble and gentle. Be patient with each other, making allowances for each other's faults because of your love. Make every effort to keep yourselves united in My Spirit, binding you together in peace (Ephesians 4:2-3 NLT).

I know you find it hard to have patience for some people but remember, patience dwells within you and My Spirit will help you to manifest it in your life. You must be in unity with others.

Father, I declare I am humble and gentle. I am patient with others and make allowances for each other's faults because of Your love in me. I will make every effort to keep myself united in the Spirit, binding myself together in peace. In Jesus' name Amen.

❖DAY 4❖
Read Galatians 5:16-26; Hebrews 6:12; Hebrews 10:36;
Romans 5:1-5; 1Timothy 6:11; John 16:33

There is a myth that if you ask Me for patience, you will have trials and tribulations in your life to give you patience. This is not true. You will have trials and tribulations in this life whether you ask Me for patience or not but I have overcome the world.

You don't have to ask Me for patience, you already have it dwelling in you. You just need to pursue it by study of My Word. Trials will help you with patience but I don't give them to you to develop your patience.

Thank You, Father, for overcoming the world so that I can endure trials and tribulations. I declare I will walk in patience. In Jesus' name Amen.

❖DAY 5❖
Read Galatians 5:16-26; Hebrews 6:12; Hebrews 10:36
Romans 5:1-5; 1Timothy 6:11; John 16:33

You are to rejoice in trials and tribulations because it will help you develop endurance. Endurance develops strength of character and character strengthens your confident hope of salvation.

I love you and I have given you My Holy Spirit to fill your hearts with My love. If you never experienced a trial, your endurance for things will not grow.

Father, it is hard to be joyful in trials but I declare I will rejoice in trials so that I can develop endurance, strength of character and confident hope of my salvation. In Jesus' name Amen.

❖DAY 6❖
Read Galatians 5:16-26; Hebrews 6:12; Hebrews 10:36
Romans 5:1-5; 1Timothy 6:11; John 16:33

Your trials are an opportunity for joy. When your faith is tested, your endurance has a chance to grow. When your endurance is fully developed, you will be perfect (mature) and complete, needing nothing.

You are not to rejoice in the troubles themselves, but in their possible results. Give thanks and praise Me in the midst of your trials and you will have the victory (Acts 16:25-34).

Father, I will see my trials for an opportunity for joy. When my faith is tested, my endurance has a chance to grow. I want my endurance to grow so that I will be perfect and complete, needing nothing. I love You Lord and praise Your holy name. In Jesus' name Amen.

❖DAY 7 – SUMMARY QUESTIONS❖
Read Galatians 5:16-26; Hebrews 6:12; Hebrews 10:36
Romans 5:1-5; 1Timothy 6:11; John 16:33

1. What is patience?

2. What are the true riches you are to pursue?

3. Where does patience dwell?

4. What is the myth about patience? What is the truth?

5. What does endurance develop?

6. What opportunity do trials give you?

NOTES:

WEEK 10
❖KINDNESS, GOODNESS, AND FAITHFULNESS❖
ﾷﾷﾷﾷﾷﾷﾷﾷﾷﾷﾷﾷﾷﾷﾷﾷﾷﾷﾷﾷﾷﾷﾷ

❖DAY 1❖
Read Galatians 5:16-26; Romans 14:17
2 Timothy 2:22

Another fruit of My Spirit is kindness which is doing a kind deed and having affection for others. It is goodness in action, having a sweet disposition while doing for others and gentleness with dealing with others. It is the ability to act in love for the welfare of those taxing your patience.

Kindness is within you because My Spirit dwells within you. Show kindness to others as I show kindness to you.

Father, I declare I will walk in the fruit of the Spirit which is kindness. I will have a sweet disposition and be gentle to those who tax my patience. In Jesus' name Amen.

❖DAY 2❖
Read Galatians 5:16-26; Romans 14:17
2 Timothy 2:22

Another fruit of My Spirit is goodness which is pretty close to kindness. It is producing a generosity and being Godlike in all your affairs.

My kingdom is living a life of goodness, peace, and joy in My Spirit which is the fruit of My Spirit that we have been talking about.

Father, I declare I will walk in the fruit of Your Spirit which is goodness and have a generous heart and be Godlike. In Jesus' name Amen.

❖DAY 3❖
Read Galatians 5:16-26; Romans 14:17
2 Timothy 2:22

Another fruit of My Spirit is faithfulness. Are you loyal and devoted to what I have called you to? Are you on time and always there to support your commitments? Faithfulness is steadfast loyalty.

My faithful love never ends. My mercies never cease. Great is My faithfulness to you and My mercies begin afresh each morning (Lamentations 3:22-23).

My mercy is My steadfast love which is linked to compassion, truth, faithfulness, and goodness. You have this steadfast love, truth, faithfulness, and goodness dwelling within you.

Thank You, Father, for Your faithfulness, mercy, compassion, truth, and goodness. It all dwells within me. I will walk in faithfulness. In Jesus' name Amen.

❖DAY 4❖
Read Galatians 5:16-26; Romans 14:17
2 Timothy 2:22

You need to run from anything that stimulates lusts and temptations. Rather, pursue righteous living, faithfulness, love and peace. You ask why you should pursue these things if they already belong to you and dwell within you?

You must pursue them because they are not automatic. Faith begins where My will is known. If you don't realize you have these things and know what they are and how they can help you, you will not know how to walk in them.

Father, I declare I will run from things of the world that stimulates lusts and temptations and pursue righteous living, faithfulness, love and peace. Thank You, Lord, that this fruit dwells within me and as I pursue them, You will manifest them in my life. In Jesus' name Amen.

46

❖DAY 5❖
Read Galatians 5:16-26; Romans 14:17
2 Timothy 2:22

Are you faithful to My Word? If you are not faithful to My Word, it will be hard to be faithful in other areas of your life. I need you to be faithful to Me and My Word.

I desire an intimacy with you that will allow Me to depend on you to be in My Word, obey it, and walk in it so you can discern My voice and answer My call on your life.

I desire such an intimacy that I can tell you what is on My heart, what I need you to pray about or where I need you to go at a certain time or day. You are called My friend if you do what I command. I no longer call you slaves, because a master doesn't confide in his slaves. Now you are my friends since I have told you everything the Father told Me (John 15:14-15).

Father, I declare I am faithful to You and to Your Word. I will meditate on Your Word, obey it, and walk in it so that I can discern Your voice and answer Your call on my life. I am Your friend and You can depend on me. In Jesus' name Amen.

❖DAY 6❖
Read Galatians 5:16-26; Romans 14:17
2 Timothy 2:22

The fruit of faithfulness is a very important attribute not just with your relationship with Me but in relationship with others. Can people depend on you to be on time or to even show up when you said you would?

That is part of being faithful; totally devoted to your commitments, to your job, to your spouse, to your children, and anyone you made a promise to. Are you sincere? If you are asked to do something and agree to it, be there. If you don't really want to do what you are asked, don't say yes to it. Faithfulness, pursue it and live it.

Father, I declare I walk in faithfulness. You and others can depend on me. I am totally devoted to my commitments and all my relationships, including You Lord. In Jesus' name Amen.

❖DAY 7 – SUMMARY QUESTIONS❖
Read Galatians 5:16-26; Romans 14:17
2 Timothy 2:22

1. What is kindness?

2. What is goodness?

3. What is faithfulness?

4. What are you to pursue? Why, if it dwells in you?

5. What does God call you?

6. What else is faithfulness?

NOTES:

WEEK 11
❖GENTLENESS AND SELF-CONTROL❖
ぞぞぞぞぞぞぞぞぞぞぞぞぞぞぞぞぞぞぞぞ

❖DAY 1❖
Read Galatians 5:16-26; 1Timothy 6:11-12
1 Peter 1:13; 2 Peter 1:3-8

Another fruit of My Spirit is gentleness. When you are walking in this fruit you have a disposition that is even-tempered, tranquil, balanced in spirit, and have your passions under control. You desire to forgive others, correct faults, and rule your spirit well.

You are My child and are to run from all evil things. Pursue righteousness and a godly life, along with faith, love, perseverance, and gentleness.

Father, I declare I have a disposition that is even-tempered, tranquil, balanced in spirit, and have my passions under control. This is the fruit of Your Spirit which is gentleness. In Jesus' name Amen.

❖DAY 2❖
Read Galatians 5:16-26; 1Timothy 6:11-12
1 Peter 1:13; 2 Peter 1:3-8

How are you to pursue righteousness, a godly life, faith, love, perseverance, and gentleness? Pursue these qualities in your life by meditating on My Word and coming into My presence. These qualities which are the fruit of My Spirit dwell within you and My Spirit will manifest them in your life when you pursue them.

You must pursue them because even though they dwell within you, they are not automatic. You must know what they are and that they are in you to have them manifest in your life.

Father, I declare I will pursue righteousness, a godly life, faith, love perseverance, gentleness, and all the fruit of Your Spirit so it will manifest in my life. In Jesus' name Amen.

❖DAY 3❖
Read Galatians 5:16-26; 1Timothy 6:11-12
1 Peter 1:13; 2 Peter 1:3-8

Another fruit of My Spirit is self-control or self-discipline. When you are walking in self-control or self-discipline you exercise restraint over your impulses, emotions, and desires. You keep your mind focused on Me and My Word so you will have good judgment, disciplined thought patterns, and the ability to understand and make right decisions.

Father, I declare I will exercise restraint over my impulses, emotions, and desires. I will keep my mind focused on You and Your Word so that I will have good judgment, disciplined thought patterns, and the ability to understand and make right decisions. In Jesus' name Amen.

❖DAY 4❖
Read Galatians 5:16-26; 1Timothy 6:11-12
1 Peter 1:13; 2 Peter 1:3-8

I have not given you a spirit of fear but of love, power and self-discipline or sound mind (2 Timothy 1:7). You seem to have a lot of fear in your life. Fear is not from Me. It is from the devil. He wants you to be in fear because when you are in fear, you do not trust Me. I have given you a spirit of power, love, self-discipline, and a sound mind.

You have My power within you. You have My love within you and you have self-discipline and a sound mind. Pursue My power, love, self-discipline, and a sound mind and they will manifest in your life.

Father, I declare I will not fear but pursue Your love, power and self-discipline and have a sound mind. In Jesus' name Amen.

❖DAY 5❖
Galatians 5:16-26; 1 Timothy 6:11-12
1 Peter 1:13; 2 Peter 1:3-8

I call you to holy living. You can do this by thinking clearly and exercising self-control. I give you a sound mind and self-control.

You are to live as My obedient children so don't slip back into your old ways of living to satisfy your own desires. You didn't know any better then but you do now and you are to be holy in everything you do. You must be holy because I am holy. My holy nature that dwells within you is the motivation for Christian holiness.

Father, I will think clearly and exercise self-control because You give me a sound mind and self-control. I will not slip back into my old ways. I will be holy in everything I do for I must be holy because You are holy. In Jesus' name Amen.

❖DAY 6❖
Galatians 5:16-26; 1 Timothy 6:11-12
1 Peter 1:13; 2 Peter 1:3-8

I have given you everything you need for living a godly life. By coming to know Me, you have received all this. I have given you great and precious promises. These promises enable you to share in My divine nature and escape the world's corruption.

You need to respond to My promises by supplementing your faith with a generous provision of moral excellence, moral excellence with knowledge, knowledge with self-control, self-control with patient endurance, patient endurance with godliness, godliness with brotherly affection, brotherly affection with love for everyone.

The more you grow in this, the more productive and useful you will be in your knowledge of Me. All this dwells within you and if you continue to pursue them, they will manifest in your life.

Father, I will respond to Your promises by supplementing my faith with moral excellence, with knowledge, self-control, patient endurance, godliness, brotherly affection, and love for everyone. I will pursue these things and grow in my knowledge of You. In Jesus' name Amen.

❖DAY 7 – SUMMARY QUESTIONS❖
Read Galatians 5:16-26; 1Timothy 6:11-12
1 Peter 1:13; 2 Peter 1:3-8

1. What is gentleness?

2. How are you to pursue righteousness, a godly life, faith, love, perseverance, and gentleness?

3. What are you exercising when you are walking in self-control?

4. What spirit has God given us? What spirit has He not given us?

5. Why must you be holy?

6. How are you to respond to God's promises?

NOTES:

WEEK 12
❖AUTHORITY IN JESUS' NAME❖
ॐॐॐॐॐॐॐॐॐॐॐॐॐ

❖DAY 1❖
Read Genesis 1:26; Luke 10:1-20

You were created to have authority in the earth but Adam and Eve turned it over to Satan by disobeying Me. I went to the cross to buy the authority Adam lost…you have authority through your union with Me.

You are joint heirs seated with Me in a heavenly place of authority (Romans 8:17; Ephesians 2:6). In Me you have been raised to the same high place of authority where I sit. The authority given to you is part of My redemptive work that I did on the cross. I became a man so you could become like Me.

Father, I declare I was created to have authority in the earth and Jesus went to the cross to buy the authority Adam lost and through my union with You, I have this authority. In Jesus' name Amen.

❖DAY 2❖
Read Genesis 1:26; Luke 10:1-20

I was sent to the earth to destroy the work of Satan and get back the authority Adam gave to him by his disobedience. I defeated Satan in hell, took from him the authority Adam had given him, and was raised to the right hand of God. I give you authority in My name over all the power and authority of Satan.

I sent the 70 disciples out two by two in My name. It's important to go out two by two rather than by yourself. They came back excited because in My name the demons were subject to them. They were amazed at what had happened. I give you that same authority in My name against the demons and against sickness and disease.

Father, I declare I have authority in Your name over all the power of Satan. In Jesus' name Amen.

❖DAY 3❖
Read Genesis 1:26; Luke 10:1-20

I saw Satan fall like lightning from heaven when the disciples defeated Satan in My name. Satan is defeated in My name. The devil only has power that you allow him to have.

Since a lot of you are not aware that you have power and authority over the devil in My name, you are defeated. You are waiting on Me to do something but I am waiting on you because I have already defeated the devil by My shed blood on the cross and I rose from the grave to give you the victory.

Father, I declare the devil is defeated in my life because of Your name and Your blood shed on the cross. You defeated him and I have the victory. In Jesus' name Amen.

❖DAY 4❖
Read Genesis 1:26; Luke 10:1-20

I have given you authority and power to trample upon serpents and scorpions, and (physical and mental strength and ability) over all the power that the enemy possesses; and nothing shall in any way harm you.

Because I give you this power and authority, you have a responsibility to use this authority I have given you. I cannot get the devil out of your life. You have My power and authority and the responsibility to command the devil out of your life. If you pray without the authority, you will not have effective prayer and the devil will defeat you.

Father, thank You for the power and authority Jesus gives me in His name. I declare I will use the name of Jesus to defeat the devil and will see him fall from heaven and have the victory. In Jesus' name Amen.

❖DAY 5❖
Read Genesis 1:26; Luke 10:1-20

I said that nothing shall in any way harm you. That should be a comfort to you with everything that is going on today. You need to believe My Word and confess that nothing shall in any way harm you.

My Spirit dwells within you. I am always there and I will protect you and keep you from harm but you must stand firm in your faith and use the power and authority I have given you to defeat the devil and the evil around you.

Father, I declare that nothing shall in any way harm me. That includes terrorists as well as sickness and disease. In Your name, I have victory over these things and over all the power that the enemy possesses. In Jesus' name Amen.

❖DAY 6❖
Read Genesis 1:26; Luke 10:1-20

You are not to rejoice in the fact that the demons are subject to the power I give you but to rejoice that your name is in the Book of life. Just knowing your name is in the Book of life and that you are enrolled in heaven should give you reason to rejoice.

Don't get prideful or think you are something great when you use My authority and power against demons and they are subject to you. You are My representative on the earth and a vessel I work through. I give you the power and authority in My name to give you the victory. The devil is under your feet and you can have the victory over him in every area of your life.

Father, I rejoice that my name is in the Book of life. I thank You that I have eternal life. I am also thankful for the power and authority in Jesus' name that is given to me to defeat the devil. I declare I will not get prideful thinking I am something great because the demons are subject to me. In Jesus' name Amen.

❖DAY 7-SUMMARY QUESTIONS❖
Read Genesis 1:26; Luke 10:1-20

1. What were you created to have in the earth?

2. What was Jesus sent to the earth to destroy?

3. How is the devil defeated?

4. What are you able to do with the authority and power in Jesus' name?

5. Can anything harm you in Jesus' name?

6. What are you to rejoice in?

NOTES:

WEEK 13
❖CAN DEMAND IN JESUS' NAME❖

❖DAY 1❖
Read John 14:12-14

I know you are probably asking how can you possibly do more than Me? It is only by My Holy Spirit working in and through you as you yield yourself to Me that you are able to do greater things.

The main emphasis of this verse is that you will be able to do all that I did (I John 4:17) I dwell within you and have given you the authority and power I had and expect you to use it and get the same results that I had when I ministered to people.

Thank You, Father, for giving me that power and authority in Jesus' name to overcome the evil in this world and be victorious. I declare I can do the things Jesus did and even greater things because the Holy Spirit lives in me. In Jesus' name Amen.

❖DAY 2❖
Read John 14:12-14

Verse 13 says I will do whatever you ask in My name. This word "ask" means demand. You can't demand anything of Me but in My name it gives you the authority to demand demons to flee, sickness to be gone, the curse to be off of your life. Because of Me you are redeemed from the curse but the devil will try to put things in your mind that are not of Me.

I give you the authority in My name to rebuke these things the devil tries to distract you with. You are not to sit back and expect Me to take care of things that I have given you the authority to handle. If you are sick, I have provided healing and in My name you are to take it and command sickness and disease to go and it will go.

Father, thank You for giving to me authority in Jesus' name to use for Your glory and have victory in my life. In Jesus' name Amen.

❖DAY 3❖
Read John 14:12-14

My name, Jesus, is above every name. Every knee will bow to My name as well as every sickness, disease, lack, etc. All authority (all power of rule) in heaven and on earth has been given to Me (Matthew 28:18) and I delegate My authority to the church and to you, and I promised you that "These signs shall follow you that believe: In My name..." (Mark 16:17).

In My name! I authorized you. I gave you My name as the authority. The power is in My name. The authority is in My name. You're authorized to use My name. Go...

Thank You, Father, for giving me the authority and power in Jesus' name in the earth. I declare I will use the authority in His name and will have the victory. In Jesus' name Amen.

❖DAY 4❖
Read John 14:12-14

I AM! I AM all that you need. By using My name you are representing all that I AM. My name represents I AM and glorifies the Father. Our Father identifies Himself as I AM WHO I AM. Revealing His divine name declares His character and attributes, reinforcing that the issue is not who you are, but who is with you and in you.

Do a study on all the names of our Father and get a better understanding of our Father God's character. My name represents the Father as I AM. All that our Father God is I AM and I have given you My name to represent our Father in the earth as I AM.

Thank You, Father, for giving me power and authority in Jesus' name, the I AM representing and glorifying You. In Jesus' name Amen.

❖DAY 5❖
Read John 14:12-14

When you use My name and take the authority I have given you in My name, it glorifies (honors and praises) our Father because you are obeying Him.

You will receive from Me what you have asked (demanded) in My name. I will do whatever you ask (demand) in My name.

Father, I want to glorify You by using Jesus' name. Thank You for Jesus and the authority in His name to use against the evil one. I declare I have authority in Jesus' name to use against the devil and the evil he tries to put on me. In Jesus' name Amen.

❖DAY 6❖
Read John 14:12-14

I said that I would grant whatever you ask in My name. Whatever you ask for? What you ask for must be what will glorify and extol our Father. You are not to ask for selfish things and things you know My Word speaks against.

Ask what is in My Word. My Word is My will. Healing is My will so you can ask for it and command sickness to be gone in My name. Sickness does not glorify our Father but healing and health does.

Father, I declare that what I ask for will glorify and extol You and Jesus will grant it to me. In Jesus' name Amen.

1. How can you do more on this earth than Jesus?

2. What does the word "ask" mean in verse 13? What does it give you?

3. What name is above every other name and what does it give you?

4. What does Jesus' name represent the Father as and what does it mean?

5. When you use Jesus' name and take the authority He has given you, what does it do?

6. Whatever you ask for must what?

NOTES:

WEEK 14
❖ARMOR OF GOD❖
❧❧❧❧❧❧❧❧❧❧❧

❖DAY 1❖
Read 2 Corinthians 10:3-6; Ephesians 6:10-18

The warfare you will battle is not of flesh and blood. It isn't against that person who is causing you trouble. It is the invisible realm that Satan works in. The weapons of warfare are not weak and worldly, they are weapons empowered by Me.

Their purpose is to demolish strongholds which is anything opposing My will. The warfare is in the mind, against arrogant rebellious ideas and attitudes (arguments) and against prideful things that are opposed to the true knowledge of Me.

Bring these thoughts into captivity to the obedience of My Word. Meditate on My Word and know it so you will be able to take captive thoughts that are not of Me.

Father, I declare I will take captive every thought that is not of You to the obedience of Christ. In Jesus' name Amen,

❖DAY 2❖
Read 2 Corinthians 10:3-6; Ephesians 6:10-18

Be strong in Me and empowered through your union with Me. You can draw your strength from Me which My authority provides.

I have provided My armor for you to protect you from the evil one. It is your responsibility to put it on! It is the armor of a heavy-armed soldier. This armor will help you successfully to stand up against the strategies and deceits of the devil and stand your ground when danger comes. You will be able to firmly stand in your place.

You are not fighting against flesh and blood but against principalities, rulers of the darkness, and spiritual hosts of wickedness in heavenly places.

Father, I declare I will put on the armor You have supplied for me so that I can resist and stand firmly in place when danger comes. In Jesus' name Amen

❖DAY 3❖
Read Ephesians 10:3-6; Ephesians 6:10-18

The first piece of armor you need to put on is the belt of truth. It is around your waist. The belt was a leather apron that secured the soldier's tunic when fighting, helped protect the body, and held the sword in place when not fighting.

In spiritual warfare, you must be living in truth. Truth is certainty, stability, rightness, trustworthiness, dependability, firmness, and reliability. You must have truth in speech and behavior. I am truth and My Word is truth. Place these attributes around your waist. If you lack righteousness and truth, it will expose you to the evil one.

The second piece of armor is the breastplate of righteousness. This provided protection from the neck to the upper part of the thighs. Truth and righteousness go together. They denote a quality of character and they stand alongside holiness. Character and conduct is effective in spiritual battle because they are My attributes that I give you.

Father, I declare I will put on the belt of truth around my waist and be dependable and reliable and have integrity. I will also put on the breastplate of righteousness and conduct myself in righteous living. Thank You, Lord, for the belt of truth and the breastplate of righteousness. In Jesus' name Amen.

❖DAY 4❖
Read 2 Corinthians 10:3-6; Ephesians 6:10-18

The third piece of armor is shoes that prepare your feet for standing firmly in battle, not necessarily for spreading the gospel. You are to be fitted with the readiness that comes from the gospel of peace. Preparation to stand unmoved against your foe, which is produced in you by My peace through My Word.

Father, I declare I will prepare my feet for readiness to stand firmly in battle that comes from Your peace and Your Word. In Jesus' name Amen.

❖DAY 5❖
Read 2 Corinthians 10:3-6; Ephesians 6:10-18

The next piece of armor is the shield of faith. Your faith and trust in Me will stand the test. Without faith, you cannot please Me. I have given everyone a measure of faith so you cannot say you do not have faith. I have given it to you. You need to develop this faith by renewing your mind to My Word.

Your faith is the shield that provides you protection from "all the flaming arrows of the evil one". All the arrows of temptation, accusations, persecution, slander, division, and deception are to be countered with faith.

Father, I declare I have on the shield of faith that will stand the test. My shield is my faith that provides protection from all the arrows from the evil one. In Jesus' name Amen.

❖DAY 6❖
Read 2 Corinthians 10:3-6; Ephesians 6:10-18

The next piece of armor is the helmet of salvation. You can be assured of your salvation in Me and know that by renewing your mind to My Word, you will be victorious in your thought life. Your mind is a major battleground in spiritual warfare. Remember, to take captive thoughts that are not of Me so the enemy will not have the opportunity to defeat you.

The sword of the Spirit is the last piece of armor. This sword is My Word. I will impart and empower the revelation of both of My written and spoken Word.

You are to attack the enemy by speaking My Word as I did in the desert by saying, "It is written". Without My Word, you cannot defeat the devil. You can defeat Satan by My blood and the Word of your testimony (the confession of My Word through your mouth) (Revelation 12:11).

Father, I declare I have on the helmet of salvation. I renew my mind to Your Word. I also have on the sword of the Spirit which is Your Word that is in my mouth and by Your blood I can overcome and be victorious. In Jesus' name Amen.

Read 2 Corinthians 10:3-6; Ephesians 6:10-18

1. The weapons of warfare are battled where and battling what?

2. What has God provided for you and what will it do?

3. What are the first two pieces of armor you must put on and what do they do?

4. What is the third piece of armor you must put on and what does it do?

5. What is the fourth piece of armor you must put on and what does it do?

6. What are the last two pieces of armor and what do they do?

NOTES:

WEEK 15
❖PRAY AND GIVE THANKS❖
❧❧❧❧❧❧❧❧❧❧❧❧❧❧❧❧❧

❖DAY 1❖
Read Ephesians 6:18; Luke 18:1
Colossians 4:2; 1 Thessalonians 5:17

Praying in the Spirit is included in the armor but not necessarily part of the armor. Prayer is actually the battle. Without prayer, you will be defeated by Satan.

Pray in the Spirit with all prayer means being led by My Spirit with different kinds of prayer such as supplication, petition, thanksgiving and also praying in tongues. Praying in tongues will empower you to stand firm and receive My revelation.

Father, I declare I will pray in the Spirit with different kinds of prayer led by Your Spirit and also pray in tongues to receive power and revelation. In Jesus' name Amen.

❖DAY 2❖
Read Ephesians 6:18; Luke 18:1
Colossians 4:2; 1 Thessalonians 5:17

You must be consistent in prayer and never give up. The enemy will try to defeat you and deceive you in believing I am not listening to your prayers nor answering your prayers.

I am always listening to you and I will always answer. I am always speaking to you but you are not always listening to Me. The noise of the world drowns out My voice. Listen for My voice. My sheep always knows My voice.

Father, I declare I will be consistent in my praying and never give up. I will not listen to the devil's lie that You are not listening to me or speaking to me. Thank You for always hearing my prayers. In Jesus' name Amen.

❖DAY 3❖
Read Ephesians 6:18; Luke 18:1
Colossians 4:2; 1 Thessalonians 5:17

Devote yourself to prayer with an alert mind and a thankful heart. You must be alert to your surroundings. Be aware of what is going on. Watch and pray. Acknowledge Me in all things so you will know what or who to pray for and how to pray in every situation.

Prayer is your first line of defense and along with all My other armor provided you will have the victory.

Father, I declare I will be devoted to prayer with an alert mind and a thankful heart. I declare I will have the victory in my life. In Jesus' name Amen.

❖DAY 4❖
Read Ephesians 6:18; Luke 18:1
Colossians 4:2; 1 Thessalonians 5:17

You must pray with a thankful heart. Be thankful in all things. I know you are asking, do you have to be thankful for all things? There is a difference between being thankful in all things and for all things. The bad things that come your way are not necessarily something to be thankful for but in the bad things you can be thankful knowing I am there with you and in the end, you will have the victory.

Be thankful in all circumstances. Praise Me in all trials and tribulations and you will receive the victory. I inhabit your praises and will strengthen you in these times of trials. Never stop praying and be thankful in (not for) every situation. This is My will for your life.

Father, I declare I will never stop praying and I will be thankful in all things because I know You will give me the victory. In Jesus' name Amen.

❖DAY 5❖
Read Ephesians 6:18; Luke 18:1
Colossians 4:2; 1 Thessalonians 5:17

When you realize that your trials and tribulations are mostly from the devil and that you will grow in Me and be strengthened when you are thankful in these times, you will have the victory in your life.

It is My will for you to be thankful in all things. My children need to have more of a grateful heart of all the things I have given them. Know that I am with you in every trial you go through and if you have a thankful heart and praise Me during these times, you will have the victory.

Father, I know most of the bad things that come my way are from the enemy and as I focus on You, I will grow and be strengthened as I give You thanks. In Jesus' name Amen.

❖DAY 6❖
Read Ephesians 6:18; Luke 18:1
Colossians 4:2; 1 Thessalonians 5:17

You need to be thankful and praise Me in the midst of trial just as Paul and Silas did when they were put in prison (Acts 16:16-34). They were beaten, put in shackles in a dark, cold stinking dungeon with rats running around. Instead of grumbling and complaining they gave thanks and lifted praises up to Me.

I got so excited because even in their situation they chose to praise Me. I started praising and twirling around along with the angels (Zephaniah 3:17). It caused the prison to shake it's foundations like an earthquake and the prison doors flew open and the shackles fell off. In the end, the jailer and his family were saved and Paul and Silas were released.

I will do the same for you if you thank Me with a grateful heart and praise Me in the midst of your trials. I inhabit your praises and sing and dance over you when you give thanks and lift praises to Me.

Father, I declare in the midst of trials I will give thanks and lift praises up to You. My shackles will be loosed and the doors will open. In Jesus' name Amen.

❖DAY 7-SUMMARY QUESTIONS❖
Read Ephesians 6:18; Luke 18:1
Colossians 4:2; 1 Thessalonians 5:17

1. What is praying in the Spirit?

2. What does the devil try to deceive you into believing?

3. What are you to devote yourself to prayer with?

4. Are you to be thankful to God for all things?

5. Who are most of your trials and tribulations from?

6. What did the Lord do when Paul and Silas gave thanks and praises to God while in prison?

NOTES:

WEEK 16
❖FRIENDSHIP WITH GOD❖
❧❧❧❧❧❧❧❧❧❧❧❧❧❧❧

❖DAY 1❖
Read Matthew 13:44-46; James 2:23-24
1 John 4:7-21; Romans 4:3; John 15:7-15

You are such a treasure to Me. You are precious to Me and I want to have fellowship with you. I paid a high price for you. I gave My all. Father sent Me to die for you to take your sins and restore fellowship with you.

I love you and want to be your friend. I am more eager for friendship with you than you are with Me. I say good things about you and that is the way I see you. If you accepted Me as your Lord and Savior, I see you righteous, without sin. See yourself as I see you.

Father, I declare I am precious to You and You treasure me. You see me as righteous and without sin and I see myself the same way. In Jesus' name Amen.

❖DAY 2❖
Read Matthew 13:44-46; James 2:23-24
1 John 4:7-21; Romans 4:3; John 15:7-15

I called Abraham My friend because he acted on his faith in Me. When he did that, his faith was completed and fulfilled. He believed in Me and it was accounted to him as righteousness. You must have faith to please Me (Hebrews 11:6; Genesis 15:6).

Faith creates actions, actions perfect faith. You are shown to be right with Me by what you do, not by faith alone. Works won't get you in right relationship with Me. You must accept Me by faith, then you will want to do things for My kingdom.

Father, I declare I am called Your friend because I act on my faith. I believe in You and it is accounted to me as righteousness just as it was for Abraham. In Jesus' name Amen.

69

❖DAY3❖
Read Matthew 13:44-46; James 2:23-24
1 John 4:7-21; Romans 4:3; John 15:7-15

You are My friend, if you do what I tell you to do.   I don't call you slaves because a master does not confide in his slaves. Now you are My friends, since I have told you everything the Father has told Me.

Draw near to Me and I will draw near to you (James 4:8). I will never leave you or forsake you (Hebrews 13:5). I love you and want to fellowship with you and tell you things to come.

Father, I will do what you tell me to do and You will call me Your friend. I will draw near to You and You will draw near to me. I love You Lord. In Jesus' name Amen.

❖DAY 4❖
Read Matthew 13:44-46; James 2:23-24
1 John 4:7-21; Romans 4:3; John 15:7-15

Did you know that friendship with the world makes you an enemy with Me. I am not of this world and to be My friend, you cannot be of this world. Your citizenship is now in heaven (Philippians 3:20). You live in this world but don't be a part of it. My Spirit will guide you and protect you as you get into My Word and seek My face.

Being My friend is a high calling. It takes time and effort to develop. You must conduct yourself according to My Word and submit to Me. Resist the devil and he will flee from you and you will have victory in your life and friendship with Me.

Father, I declare I do not have friendship with the world because that makes me an enemy with You. I am not of this world because You are not of this world. My citizenship is in heaven. In Jesus' name Amen.

❖DAY 5❖
Read Matthew 13:44-46; James 2:23-24
1 John 4:7-21; Romans 4:3; John 15:7-15

I am love and love dwells within you. Since I loved you and love dwells in you, you must love one another. There is no fear in My love because perfect love casts out fear. Fear brings torment. If you are in fear, you have not experienced My perfect love. Put your trust in My love and friendship. I am for you, not against you.

If you say you love Me, you must love others. You cannot love Me if you do not love your brothers and sisters.

Father, I declare Your love dwells in me, I will love others. There is no fear in Your love so I will not fear and I will trust Your love and friendship. In Jesus' name Amen.

❖DAY 6❖
Read Matthew 13:44-46; James 2:23-24
1 John 4:7-21; Romans 4:3; John 15:7-15

I am a friend that sticks closer than a brother. I am with you always and will never leave you. Abide in Me and in My Word and you shall have what you ask for. Take up residence in My love. You will never be without My love.

You will abide in My love if you obey My commandments. Natural friendships can sometimes be complicated but friendship with Me will only give you an advantage.

Get a revelation of how much I love you and want to fellowship with you. You are precious to Me and I am waiting for you to fellowship with Me. You can come boldly to Me, no matter what is going on in your life. You think you are nothing but you are everything to Me. Come to Me and let Me show you My love and friendship.

Father, I declare You are a friend that sticks closer than a brother. You are always with me and will never leave me. I abide in You and Your Word and receive what I ask for. I obey You and abide in Your love. Give me a revelation of Your awesome love and friendship. In Jesus' name Amen.

Read Matthew 13:44-46; James 2:23-24
1 John 4:7-21; Romans 4:3; John 15:7-15

1. Jesus wants to be your what?

2. Why did God call Abraham His friend?

3. We are His friend because of what?

4. What does friendship with this world cause? Where is your citizenship?

5. What will cast out fear? What does fear bring?

6. What kind of friend is Jesus? How do you abide in His love?

NOTES:

WEEK 17
❖BLESSING OF ABRAHAM❖
ഛഛഛഛഛഛഛഛഛഛഛഛഛ

❖DAY 1❖
Read Genesis 1:28-31; Genesis 12:1-3; Genesis 9:1-2
Galatians 3:13-16; Deuteronomy 28

Adam and Eve were told to be fruitful and multiply. Fill the earth and govern it. Reign over the fish in the sea, the birds in the sky and all the animals that scurry along the ground. They were given every seed bearing tree for food for them and the animals. This blessing gave them the responsibility and the resources to fill the earth with My goodness. They messed that blessing up by being disobedient to My Word and turned it all over to Satan. The curse was on the earth because of their sin.

I gave the same blessing to Noah after the flood. They were to go replenish the earth. I had placed everything in his power. It was through the bloodline of Shem, one of Noah's sons, that Abram was born. The blessing was restored to Abram (Abraham).

Father, all through the ages You have tried to restore the blessing to us. As long as we obey You and Your Word, the blessing is on us. Thank You for the blessing. In Jesus' name Amen.

❖DAY 2❖
Read Genesis 1:28-31; Genesis 12:1-3; Genesis 9:1-2
Galatians 3:13-16; Deuteronomy 28

Abraham was called My friend because he believed My promise and walked his faith out. Sure, he failed a time or two, but by his faith he was counted righteous in My eyes and because of this, you became a child of Abraham, an heir to the blessing. When he was counted as righteous, it was for your benefit as well as his, assuring you that I will also count you as righteous, if you believe in Me.

Father, I declare I am Your friend because I believe You and walk in faith. I am counted as righteous because of my faith in Jesus. In Jesus' name Amen.

❖DAY 3❖
Read Genesis 1:28-31; Genesis 12:1-3; Genesis 9:1-2
Galatians 3:13-16; Deuteronomy 28

Adam's blessing and Abraham's blessing are the same. It was Abraham's faith and his covenant with Me that made the way for Me to come to earth. My birth, life, ministry, sacrifice for your sin, and My resurrection were all possible because Abraham believed and received the blessing, not just for himself, but for his Seed.

I came to get the blessing back for all nations, to demonstrate its true power and make it available again to every man, woman and child on earth who would put their faith in Me. I came to release and restore the power of the blessing.

Thank You, Father, for the blessing that is given to me through Jesus Christ. I can live in the blessing and have dominion on the earth through Jesus. In Jesus' name Amen.

. ❖DAY 4❖
Read Genesis 1:28-31; Genesis 12:1-3; Genesis 9:1-2
Galatians 3:13-16; Deuteronomy 28

I have redeemed you from the curse that came when Adam and Eve disobeyed our Father when I went to the cross. I became the curse for you. You have been redeemed from sickness, poverty, lack, and all that the devil put on this earth. He no longer has control on this earth or in you.

You now have dominion to rule the earth, be fruitful and multiply, reign over the fish in the sea, the birds in the sky, and all the animals that scurry along the ground. You have the responsibility and the resources to fill the earth with My goodness. The only authority the devil has is what you give to him. Resist him and he will flee from you.

Thank You, Father, for sending Jesus to redeem me from the curse. Thank You for the dominion and authority that I have. In Jesus' name Amen.

❖DAY 5❖
Read Genesis 1:28-31; Genesis 12:1-3; Genesis 9:1-2
Galatians 3:13-16; Deuteronomy 28

The blessings mentioned in Deuteronomy 28 and in many other places in My Word are all yours if you accepted Me as your Lord and Savior. Since you are righteous because of My sacrifice on the cross, even when you mess up, these blessings are still yours.

You still need to be obedient to My Word but the blessings are yours. You need to know what these blessings are so you can claim them as yours and walk in them.

Father, I declare I have all the blessings that You mention in Deuteronomy 28 as well as all the blessings in Your Word. I will find out what they are and claim them and walk in them. In Jesus' name Amen.

❖DAY 6❖
Read Genesis 1:28-31; Genesis 12:1-3; Genesis 9:1-2
Galatians 3:13-16; Deuteronomy 28

You have been redeemed from the curse of the law. All the curses in Deuteronomy 28 you are redeemed from. You do not have to struggle with these things. You must know what you are redeemed from to walk free of them.

My Spirit dwells in you to guide you into all truth. Walk in My Spirit, not your flesh. When you walk in the flesh, you get into trouble, sin, sickness, and lack comes knocking at your door. Walking in My Spirit is not hard. You make it harder than it is. My yoke is easy (Matthew 11:28-30) but you push and pull against it making it hard. Don't struggle, go with the flow and you will be blessed.

You need to be walking in the blessing so others will see and want what you have. They will seek you out to know how to receive what you have.

Father, I declare I am redeemed from the curse and walk in the blessings You have given me as a child of Yours. I declare Your yoke is easy and I will not make it harder than it is to walk in Your Spirit. In Jesus' name Amen.

Read Genesis 1:28-31; Genesis 12:1-3; Genesis 9:1-2
Galatians 3:13-16; Deuteronomy 28

1. What was Adam and Eve told to do? What happened?

2. You became what when Abraham was counted righteous before God because of his faith?

3. What made the way for Jesus to come to the earth?

4. What has Jesus redeemed us from and what has it given you?

5. What are the blessings from Deuteronomy 28 that are yours?

6. What causes you to get into trouble and have the curse knocking at your door? What are these curses?

NOTES:

WEEK 18
❖GOODNESS OF GOD❖
❧❧❧❧❧❧❧❧❧❧❧❧❧

❖DAY 1❖
Read Psalm 84:11; Psalm 34:8-10
Psalm 145:8-9; Psalm 100; Matthew 6:25-34

There is a song out there that a lot of My children are singing called "Good, Good Father" by Chris Tomlin but do you really believe what you are singing. It says, "You're a good, good Father. It's who You are. And I am loved by You, it's who I am".

Do you really believe that I am a good Father? If so, why do you complain so much? Do you realize how much I love you? You wouldn't be blaming Me for the bad things happening in your life if you realized how much I loved you. Don't doubt My love or My goodness.

Father, I declare You are a good, good Father to me and that You love me more than I can even imagine. Thank You for being good to me. In Jesus' name Amen.

❖DAY 2❖
Read Psalm 84:11; Psalm 34:8-10
Psalm 145:8-9; Psalm 100; Matthew 6:25-34

I am the light shining in your darkness and I protect you with a shield around you. I give you grace, favor and My glory which is everything good.

I will never withhold anything good from you. The bad things happening in your life are not from Me. Satan loves to deceive you just as he did Eve in the garden (Genesis 1:1-6). He made Me sound like I was withholding things from them. They listened to him and sin entered into the world. You do the same thing. Trust My goodness.

Father, I declare You are a light shining in my darkness and protecting me with a shield around me. I have Your grace, favor, and everything good in my life. I will not be deceived by Satan who tries to tell me that You withhold good things from me. In Jesus 'name Amen.

❖DAY 3❖
Read Psalm 84:11; Psalm 34:8-10
Psalm 145:8-9; Psalm 100; Matthew 6:25-34

You need to taste (discern) and see that I am good to you. You are blessed if you trust Me. You are to fear (reverence) Me for there is no lack for those who fear Me.

If you seek Me, search Me out, research the Word about My love and goodness, you will not lack any good thing. When you seek Me, you will find Me and My goodness will be poured out on you.

Father, I declare I taste and see that You are good to me. I declare I fear You and I am blessed because I trust You. I will seek You and Your Word about Your love and goodness to me. I will not lack any good thing. In Jesus' name Amen.

❖DAY 4❖
Read Psalm 84:11; Psalm 34:8-10
Psalm 145:8-9; Psalm 100; Matthew 6:25-34

Put your faith in Me. Believe that I am good. I know when you trust Me and take refuge in Me. When trouble comes I will be a strong refuge for you and be close to you (Nahum 1:7).

I am good to you and will shower compassion on you when you stumble and fail. My love and goodness will never fail you. If a natural father desires good gifts to his children, how much more will I give good gifts to you? I will never put bad in your life. If you are experiencing bad things in your life, you either disobeyed Me or you allowed Satan a foothold in your life. Believe that I am good.

Father, I declare I put my faith in You and believe that You are good. When trouble comes, You will be a strong refuge for me and stay close to me because You know I trust You. I will not blame You for the bad things in my life. In Jesus' name Amen.

❖DAY 5❖
Read Psalm 84:11; Psalm 34:8-10
Psalm 145:8-9; Psalm 100; Matthew 6:25-34

Shout with joy to Me. Worship Me with gladness. Come into My presence, singing with joy. When you do, I will sing songs of deliverance over you and bring victory in your life. Acknowledge that I am God. I created you and you are mine. You are My people, the sheep of My pasture.

Enter My presence with thanksgiving and with praise. Give thanks to Me and praise My name. Do this because I am good. My unfailing love and faithfulness continues forever.

Father, I declare I will shout with joy to You and worship You with gladness. Thank You for singing songs of deliverance to me. I will enter Your presence with thanksgiving and with praise. You are good and Your unfailing love and faithfulness continues forever. In Jesus' name Amen.

❖DAY 6❖
Read Psalm 84:11; Psalm 34:8-10
Psalm 145:8-9; Psalm 100; Matthew 6:25-34

I don't want you to worry about anything in your life. Worry won't change a thing and it is a sin. I will take care of everything in your life as long as you seek Me and My righteousness first.

I know what you need and want to give these things to you. I am a good, good Father and take care of My children. Seek Me and you will find Me and all that you need.

Father, I declare I will not worry about anything but seek You and Your righteousness. You will give me all I need and take care of me because You are a good, good Father and love me. In Jesus' name Amen.

79

❖DAY 7-SUMMARY QUESTIONS❖
Read Psalm 84:11; Psalm 34:8-10
Psalm 145:8-9; Psalm 100; Matthew 6:25-34

1. Do you believe God is a good, good Father and loves you more than you can imagine?

2. Are the bad things that are happening in your life from God? Who are they from?

3. What will happen when you seek the Lord?

4. When trouble comes, what will God be for you?

5. How are you to enter God's presence?

6. God will take care of everything in your life when you do what?

NOTES:

WEEK 19
❖THE LORD IS YOUR SHEPHERD❖
〜〜〜〜〜〜〜〜〜〜〜〜〜〜〜〜〜〜〜〜

❖DAY 1❖
Read Psalm 23; John 10:1-16

I am your good shepherd. I will feed, guide, and protect you from all harm. I cherish you. You have all that you need. If you recognize My voice and follow after Me, you will know Satan's voice and not be deceived.

I will lead you. I do not push or drive you. You are My sheep which follow the shepherd unlike cattle that have to be driven. The devil will push you into decisions.

I give you an abundant life. Satan comes to steal, kill, and destroy. So remember, if bad things are in your life, Satan was given an open door to your life. I will give you the victory to overcome by My blood and the word of your testimony. I have also given you authority in My name against evil in your life.

Father, I declare You are my good shepherd and I have all that I need. I recognize Your voice and will follow after You. I will not follow after Satan's voice and be deceived. Thank You that I can overcome and have victory in my life. In Jesus' name Amen.

❖DAY 2❖
Read Psalm 23; John 10:1-16

You will lie down in fresh, tender green pastures. This means you will be safe in Me. In the midst of the storms and noise in your life, I will lead you to waters of rest and quietness.

You can enter into this rest through salvation in Me. In Me is rest, peace, and quietness. In the secret place (Psalm 91:1) is where you will find My rest. Come and remain in Me (John 15:1-8).

Father, I declare I will lie down in fresh green pastures. I am safe in You. I have entered into this rest because You are my Lord and Savior. I dwell in the secret place and remain in You. In Jesus' name Amen.

❖DAY 3❖
Read Psalm 23; John 10:1-16

Walk in My wisdom and discernment, they will refresh your soul and keep you safe on your journey (Proverbs 3:22-23).

I will renew your strength and guide you along the right path which brings honor to Me. As you follow Me, you will walk in righteousness, which is right standing with Me.

Father, I declare I will walk in Your wisdom and discernment. They will refresh my soul and keep me safe. You renew my strength and guide me on righteous paths that give You honor. In Jesus' name Amen.

❖DAY 4❖
Read Psalm 23; John 10:1-16

When you walk through the darkest valley and are overcome by evil, you do not have to be afraid. You feel sometimes a dark cloud is hanging over you and there is no way out from under it. Do not be afraid, I am close beside you. I will protect, guide, and comfort you.

When you have lost a loved one, I am there with you, comforting you and giving you peace. My glory light that is within you will shine bright and cause the darkness to flee. You are protected by the shadow of My wings so the shadow of death will not overtake you. Trust in Me and the glory light that is within you to penetrate the darkness.

Father, I declare I will not fear when I feel a dark cloud over me. Your glory light that shines within me will cause the darkness to flee. I trust You and Your glory light to always shine in the darkness and it cannot overtake me. In Jesus' name Amen.

❖DAY 5❖
Read Psalm 23; John 10:1-16

I pour out blessings upon you in the presence of your enemies. Unbelievers are watching you so walk in My Spirit so that they will desire what you have.

Many will come to you asking about your blessings and the light that shines from you. You will be able to tell them about Me and what I can do for them. Always be aware of those around you. Walk in My Spirit, not the flesh.

Father, I declare You pour out blessings upon me in the presence of my enemies. I will walk in Your Spirit and let Your light shine in the darkness. People will see my blessings and Your light and want what I have. In Jesus' name Amen.

❖DAY 6❖
Read Psalm 23; John 10:1-16

I will lead you with My unfailing love and goodness all the days of your life. Blessings will overflow in your life. My presence is with you and in you.

Receive the revelation of My presence, love and power dwelling in you and through you. Without my presence, you will not be aware of My goodness and My blessings so stay in My presence, stay in My Word so you can receive revelation of things to come. I love you and want you to walk in all that I have for you.

Father, I declare I am led by Your unfailing love and goodness all the days of my life and that blessings will overflow in my life. As long as I stay in Your presence, I will walk in all that You have for me. In Jesus' name Amen.

Read Psalm 23; John 10:1-16

1. Who is the good shepherd? What does the good shepherd do for you?

2. What does lying down in fresh green pastures mean?

3. What does Jesus' wisdom and discernment give you?

4. What will cause the dark cloud in your life to flee?

5. God will pour out blessings upon you in the presence of whom?

6. God will lead you with what and how often?

NOTES:

WEEK 20
❖ YOU ARE SALT AND LIGHT ❖
❧❧❧❧❧❧❧❧❧❧❧❧❧❧❧❧

❖ DAY 1 ❖
Read Matthew 5:13-16; John 3:16-21
Psalm 119:130

You are the salt of the earth. What do I mean by salt? Salt is a seasoning and preserving agent. What I mean by being the salt of the earth is that when you speak to others, your speech is encouraging and helpful (Colossians 4:6).

Your conduct and speech is to preserve those around you to bring peace into any situation. Only through Me can your salt remain salty so stay in My Word and focused on Me. Otherwise, the salt will lose its flavor and you will be worthless in My kingdom.

Father, I declare I am the salt of the earth encouraging others through the words I speak and conducting myself in a way that preserves those around me bringing Your peace into the situation and my relationships. In Jesus' name Amen.

❖ DAY 2 ❖
Read Matthew 5:13-16; John 3:16-21
Psalm 119:130

You also are the light of the world like a city on a hilltop that cannot be hidden. I am light and I came into the world but people loved the darkness more than the light, for their actions were evil. My light exposes their evil so they stay in the darkness.

You do right and have come to My light. This light is My glory and it dwells within you. Everywhere you go, let My light shine so others can see Your blessings.

Father, I declare I am the light of the world because Your glory dwells in me and I will let Your glory shine forth into the darkness. In Jesus' name Amen.

❖DAY 3❖
Read Matthew 5:13-16; John 3:16-21
Psalm 119:130

Adam and Eve were crowned/covered with My glory. When they sinned, My glory was removed and they saw their nakedness. This is what it means when I say in My Word that you have fallen short of My glory (Romans 3:23). I have crowned you with My glory when you accepted Me as your Lord and Savior.

Moses asked to see My glory and I put him in the cleft of the rock with My hand covering him. I removed My hand as I walked by and he could see My backside.

He went down from My presence and had to put a veil over his face because of the brightness of My glory. My glory is the light of My goodness. My glory that is in you needs to be released not covered.

Thank You, Father, for crowning me and covering me with Your glory that shines from me. In Jesus' name Amen.

❖DAY 4❖
Read Matthew 5:13-16; John 3:16-21
Psalm 119:130

My glory is My splendor, radiance, majesty, absolute perfection, honor, power, wealth, authority, fame, dignity, and excellency. My glory is in you (John 17:21-24).

You need to release My glory into the atmosphere. How do you do that? You must realize My glory is in you before you can release it. You have all things you need in you for life and godliness (2 Peter 1:3).

Father, I declare Your glory and all that I need for life and godliness dwells in me and I will release it into the atmosphere. In Jesus' name Amen.

❖DAY 5❖
Read Matthew 5:13-16; John 3:16-21
Psalm 119:130

You don't need to ask Me to pour out or send My glory in Your life or your churches or into the darkness because I have already poured out My glory on you and in you when you accepted Me.

When you get that revelation that My glory is poured out in you and on you, you will become a lighthouse or beacon shining out clearly in the darkness (Philippians 2:13-16). All that My glory represents is in you to be released in the world around you.

Father, I declare Your glory is in me and I will release Your glory out from within me so that I will be a beacon shining out clearly in the darkness. In Jesus' name Amen.

❖DAY 6❖
Read Matthew 5:13-16; John 3:16-21
Psalm 119:130

What does My glory do in you? It gives you great creative power to know My glory and shines out to others. You have this light shining in your heart and it is there to help in your troubles and to shine out to others (2 Corinthians 4:1-18).

My glory in you will meet your needs and will display My riches. Get into My Word, meditate in it continually and it will give you light, for My Word is a lamp to guide you and a light for your path.

My glory is My presence and is always in you and with you. I crown you with My glory and cover you. Let others see My glory. If all believers received the revelation of My glory that is in them, mighty miracles would happen.

Father, I declare Your glory gives me great creative power to know Your glory and I will shine it out in the darkness. I declare Your glory meets my needs and gives me riches because You live in me. I will meditate on Your Word and receive light to guide me. I will release Your glory into the darkness so that others will come to the light. Miracles will manifest wherever Your glory shines out. In Jesus' name Amen.

❖DAY 7-SUMMARY QUESTIONS❖
Read Matthew 5:13-16; John 3:16-21
Psalm 119:130

1. What does being salt of the earth mean?

2. You are light of this world. What is this light?

3. What is the light of God's glory?

4. How do you release God's glory into the atmosphere?

5. Where is God's glory?

6. What does God's glory do in you?

NOTES:

WEEK 21
❖YOU ARE HEALED❖
❀❀❀❀❀❀❀❀❀❀❀❀

❖DAY 1❖
Read Isaiah 53:4-5; Matthew 8:17
1 Peter 2:24; Psalm 103:3

I want you to know that healing was provided in My atonement on the cross just as much as your sins were forgiven. I took your pain and bore your sickness and by My stripes that were laid on My back you were made whole.

The faith you had to accept Me as your Lord and Savior is the same faith you need to be healed. I am willing and able to heal you.

Father, I declare that You took my pain and bore my sicknesses and by Your stripes I am healed and made whole. Thank You Lord. In Jesus' name Amen.

❖DAY 2❖
Read Isaiah 53:4-5; Matthew 8:17
1 Peter 2:24; Psalm 103:3

I know you think that the pain and sickness you are experiencing is from Me. I heal and bring life, the devil comes to steal, kill and destroy (John 10:10).

I do not teach My children with sickness and pain. I teach by My Word (2 Timothy 3:16). You must believe to receive. I have given you My Word and My authority against any attacks from the enemy to be victorious. Walk in My Spirit, not the flesh. Your flesh will tell you that you are not healed but believe My Word that says that you are healed.

Father, I declare You bring healing and life to me. The devil comes to steal, kill, and destroy. I take authority over the devil and declare I am healed. In Jesus' name Amen.

89

❖DAY 3❖
Read Isaiah 53:4-5; Matthew 8:17
1 Peter 2:24; Psalm 103:3

All sickness is from the devil (Acts 10:38). When I was on the earth I went around preaching the Word and healing all that were oppressed by the enemy. I never told anyone it wasn't the Father's will to heal them. I healed all who came to Me.

I am willing and able to heal all. Actually, once you accepted Me as Your Lord and Savior, My Spirit and all that comes with Him, came to dwell within you. So, healing is in you. You just need to learn how to release it from your spirit into the natural.

You do that by renewing your mind to My Word that says I took your pain and bore your sicknesses. I am the Lord that heals you (Exodus 15:26).

Father, I declare all sickness is from the devil and it is Your will to heal me. You are the God that heals me. In Jesus' name Amen.

❖DAY 4❖
Read Isaiah 53:4-5; Matthew 8:17
1 Peter 2:24; Psalm 103:3

There are many verses in My Word that tell you about My healing power, especially how I ministered to people when I was on the earth. I came to save you, heal you and deliver you from the oppression of the devil. He is defeated and you have the victory but you must renew your mind to My Word because the devil doesn't give up.

He can only do to you what you allow him to do because I have given you the authority over him. Humble yourself before Me. Resist the devil and he shall flee from you (James 4:7). You must resist him. I cannot resist him for you or tell him to flee. I have given you that authority in My name.

Father, I declare I will meditate on Your Word regarding healing to renew my mind. I will humble myself before You and resist the devil and he shall flee. In Jesus' name Amen.

❖DAY 5❖
Read Isaiah 53:4-5; Matthew 8:17
1 Peter 2:24; Psalm 103:3

Always remember and give Me praise for all I have done for you. I have forgiven you of all your sins, I have provided healing power for you today to be totally healed and whole, I have redeemed your life from destruction, crowned you with love and tender mercies. I fill your life with good things and renew your strength.

Healing of your body was provided on the cross just as forgiveness of your sins. Receive your healing just the same way you received salvation.

Father, I will remember and give You praise for all that You have done for me and what You have provided for me on the cross. I declare I am forgiven of all my sins, I am healed of all my diseases, and my strength is renewed. Thank You Lord. In Jesus' name Amen.

❖DAY 6❖
Read Isaiah 53:4-5; Matthew 8:17
1 Peter 2:24; Psalm 103:3

Take note, I have forgiven all of your sins and healed all of your diseases. All means ALL. I have made salvation and healing easy for people but they make it harder than it is and when you receive Me, healing is included. You receive healing by faith the same way you receive salvation.

If you accepted Me as your Lord and Savior, healing is in you. You've already got it. It dwells within you. You just need to renew your mind, realize it is there, and receive it by faith.

I am the God who heals you. I want you to walk in divine health and it is available to you. Walk in My Spirit, not the flesh and you will have the victory.

Father, I declare all my sins are forgiven and all my diseases are healed. I will walk in the Spirit and walk in faith. I declare You are my healer and I receive my healing by faith. In Jesus' name Amen.

91

❖DAY 7-SUMMARY QUESTIONS❖
Read Isaiah 53:4-5; Matthew 8:17
1 Peter 2:24; Psalm 103:3

1. What did Jesus take on the cross?

2. Does God teach us with sickness and pain?

3. Where does sickness come from?

4. What must you do to defeat the devil?

5. How do you receive your healing?

6. How many of your sins has Jesus forgiven and how many diseases has Jesus healed?

NOTES:

WEEK 22
❖YOU ARE PROTECTED❖
❧❧❧❧❧❧❧❧❧❧❧❧❧❧

❖DAY 1❖
Read Psalm 91; 1 Peter 1:5

As with all of My promises, there are conditions that apply. Even though you have accepted Me as Your Lord and Savior, if you are not in the secret place, you will not have rest and protection.

If you are directed by the Holy Spirit to go a certain direction and you go a different direction and get into an accident, you cannot blame Me for not protecting you. That is why you were directed a different way, to protect you.

It's a matter of listening to the leading of the Holy Spirit and being obedient to that leading. You must stay in the secret place, make Me your refuge, trust and lean on Me. I can then deliver you from every trap and protect you from deadly diseases.

Father, I declare I am in the secret place and I make You my refuge and trust in You. Thank You for delivering me from every trap and protecting me from deadly diseases. In Jesus' name Amen.

❖DAY 2❖
Read Psalm 91; 1 Peter 1:5

The secret place is My presence. You must remain in Me. The secret place is not a place you can come and go you must remain. As the branch is connected to the vine, you must stay connected to Me. It is a lifestyle.

This lifestyle is walking in My Spirit, not your flesh. Renewing your mind to My Word and being obedient to what My Word says.

Father, I declare I will remain in You. I will stay connected to You by walking in Your Spirit, renewing my mind to Your Word and being obedient to Your Word. In Jesus' name Amen.

93

❖DAY 3❖
Read Psalm 91; 1 Peter 1:5

The enemy will try to trap you but I will rescue you and protect you from all accusations. My protective arms are wrapped around you. Run under My covering. I am faithful to keep you from harm.

Do not fear at night because I never sleep and will watch over you to keep you safe. I give you sweet sleep (Psalm 3:5; 4:8).

Father, I declare You will rescue me from every trap the enemy places before me. You will protect me from all accusations. Your protective arms are wrapped around me, covering me and keeping me from harm. I will not fear at night or in the darkness because You never sleep and watch over me to keep me safe from harm. Thank You for giving me sweet sleep and wake up refreshed. In Jesus' name Amen.

❖DAY 4❖
Read Psalm 91; 1 Peter 1:5

You will be a spectator as the wicked perish in judgment, for they will be paid back for what they have done. Vengeance is mine (Romans 12:19).

When you live your life in My shadow or presence, I will always shield you from harm. No evil or disease can prevail against you (Isaiah 54:17).

Father, I declare I will be a spectator as the wicked perish in judgment. Vengeance is Yours and they will be paid back for what they have done. I will live in Your presence and be shielded from harm. No evil or disease can prevail against me. In Jesus' name Amen.

❖DAY 5❖
Read Psalm 91; 1 Peter 1:5

I will send angels with special orders to protect you wherever you go. They will keep you from stumbling when you walk into a trap.

You will trample every power of darkness under your feet and walk unharmed. I also give you authority in My name to come against the evil one. Resist the devil and he will flee from you (James 4:7).

Father, thank You for the angels You send to protect me wherever I go. I will trample every power of darkness under my feet and will walk unharmed. I will use the authority in Jesus' name against the devil and he will flee from me. In Jesus' name Amen.

❖DAY 6❖
Read Psalm 91; 1 Peter 1:5

As you delight in Me and remain in My presence, I will greatly protect you and set you in a high place, safe and secure before Me. I will always answer your cry for help. You will find and feel My presence in times of trouble. I will rescue and honor you.

I will satisfy you with long life and you will enjoy the fullness of My salvation. You are My child and I love you and will keep you safe from harm. By your faith, My mighty power will constantly guard you.

Father, I declare I delight in You and will remain in Your presence. As I do, You will protect me and set me in a high place, safe and secure before You. You will always answer my cry for help. I will find and feel Your presence in times of trouble. You will rescue and honor me. You will satisfy me with long life and I will enjoy the fullness of Your salvation. As I walk in faith, You will constantly guard me. In Jesus' name Amen.

Read Psalm 91; 1 Peter 1:5

1. Where must you stay and who should you trust to be protected and kept safe?

2. What is the secret place?

3. Where are God's protective arms? What does God give you at night?

4. Vengeance belongs to whom?

5. God will send what to protect you?

6. What will God satisfy you with? It's by your WHAT that God's power will constantly guard you?

NOTES:

WEEK 23
❖FREE IN CHRIST❖
❧❧❧❧❧❧❧❧❧❧❧

❖DAY 1❖
Read John 8:36; Galatians 5:1, 13
2 Corinthians 3:17; Luke 4:18-19

When you embrace the truth of My Word, you prove you are My true followers. When you embrace My truth, it releases more freedom into your life.

What do I mean by freedom? What are you free from? The truth I give you releases you from the bondage of your past, the bondage of your sins, and the bondage of religion. Truth must be embraced and worked out through the divine process of spiritual maturity, renewing your mind to My Word. The Greek word for "truth" is *reality*. To embrace reality in Me brings more freedom into your life.

Father, I declare I will embrace the truth of Your Word and prove that I am a true follower. Thank You for the freedom You give to me by embracing Your truth. In Jesus' name Amen.

❖DAY 2❖
Read John 8:36; Galatians 5:1, 13
2 Corinthians 3:17; Luke 4:18-19

When you sin you become a slave to sin. In Me, sin has no more dominion over you and you have become a child of God, no longer a slave.

So if I have set you free, you are unquestionably free and are a true child of God. You are free, no longer a slave to sin.

Thank You, Father, for setting me free from sin so that I am no longer a slave to sin. Jesus has set me free so I am free indeed. In Jesus' name Amen.

❖DAY 3❖
Read John 8:36; Galatians 5:1, 13
2 Corinthians 3:17; Luke 4:18-19

Since I have completely liberated you, do not submit again to a yoke of slavery. It is only through My Spirit that you walk in Godliness. It is not achieved by observing external codes. Any attempt to achieve righteousness through a list of dos and don'ts is fruitless.

Walk in the freedom I have purchased for you. You have been called to liberty but don't use it for the flesh and selfishness. You are to serve one another in love as I have loved you.

Father, I declare You have completely liberated me, I will not submit again to a yoke of slavery. It is only through the Holy Spirit that I walk in Godliness. It is not achieved by external lists of dos and don'ts. I will walk in the freedom You have purchased for me and not allow my flesh any freedom. In Jesus' name Amen.

❖DAY 4❖
Read John 8:36; Galatians 5:1, 13
2 Corinthians 3:17; Luke 4:18-19

When you turn to Me, the veil or darkness is taken away. I am the Spirit and wherever My Spirit is, there is freedom.

My Spirit dwells in you so you can walk in freedom. You can see and reflect My glory. I will make you more and more like Me as you are changed into My glorious image. You are free from darkness, bondage, sickness, lack, and oppression. You are free in Me.

Father, I have turned to You and the veil is removed. Wherever Your Spirit is, there is freedom. I walk in freedom and can see and reflect Your glory. I am changing into Your glorious image. I am free in Christ. Thank You Lord. In Jesus' name Amen.

❖DAY 5❖
Read John 8:36; Galatians 5:1, 13
2 Corinthians 3:17; Luke 4:18-19

The Spirit is upon Me. I was anointed to bring Good News to the poor. Are you poor? I have freedom for you to prosper you and set you free from lack.

Father has sent Me to proclaim that captives or prisoners will be released. Do you feel you are in a prison? You are set free in Me. The blind will see, not just physically but spiritually, you will see.

The oppressed and depressed will be set free. You no longer need to be oppressed of the devil or depressed about anything. I have set you free. My favor is upon you to deliver you.

Father, I declare that You have brought Good News to the poor and that I can prosper. You have set me free from prison. The blind will see. You open my eyes to see the revelation of Your Word. I am set free from depression and no longer oppressed by the devil. Your favor is upon me. Thank You Lord. In Jesus' name Amen.

❖DAY 6❖
Read John 8:36; Galatians 5:1, 13
2 Corinthians 3:17; Luke 4:18-19

This anointing is not just on Me but it is on you if you have accepted Me. I send you out to bring Good News to the poor. You are to proclaim freedom to the captives and prisoners of the evil one.

You are to set the blind free so they can see and set the oppressed and depressed free. My favor is on you to give to others to be delivered and set free.

Father, I declare I am anointed to bring Good News to the poor, to proclaim freedom to the captives and prisoners of the evil one. I am to set the blind free by Your anointing that is upon me and give favor to others to be delivered. Thank You for Your anointing that is in me and on me. In Jesus' name Amen.

Read John 8:36; Galatians 5:1, 13
2 Corinthians 3:17; Luke 4:18-19

1. What happens when you embrace the truth of the Lord? What is freedom? What is truth?

2. In Christ, what have you become and what are you set free from?

3. How do you walk in Godliness?

4. What is taken away when we turn to Jesus?

5. What does the anointing of God give to us through Jesus?

6. What does God send us out to do through His anointing?

NOTES:

WEEK 24
❖MEMBERS OF CHRIST'S BODY❖

❖DAY 1❖
Read 1 Corinthians 12:2-27; Romans 12:4-5
Ephesians 4:16

Each part of the body is unique and each part is just as important as any other part. You can't say to the ear, "I have no need of you" or to the hand, "I have no need of you" or to the weaker parts of the body, "that I have no need of you".

You need to stop comparing yourself to other people and where they are in ministry, their personalities, or how they look. You are just as important and unique as the other person.

Father, I declare I am unique and just as important in the body as any other person. I will stop comparing myself to other people. In Jesus' name Amen.

❖DAY 2❖
Read 1 Corinthians 12:2-27; Romans 12:4-5
Ephesians 4:16

I have adjusted, mingled together in harmony, and proportioned the parts of the whole body to where I want you, giving greater honor and richer endowment to the inferior parts which lack apparent importance (Verse. 24 Amplified). You are all important and should have no division or discord.

I compare My body to a puzzle. Each piece fits in a specific spot. If you try to put a piece in the wrong spot, it will not fit and the puzzle will not come out right. You can't force a puzzle piece to go into a spot it doesn't fit in. You should not try to fit in a position I have not called you to or be like someone else.

Father, I declare I am important and should not have any division or discord in the body. I fit in the body in a special place You have for me just as each piece of a puzzle fits in a special place. In Jesus' name Amen.

101

❖DAY 3❖
Read 1 Corinthians 12:2-27; Romans 12:4-5
Ephesians 4:16

I assign a piece of a puzzle to each one of you. Each piece is shaped different and fits differently. Each person has a different function and is unique to Me.

The position I have placed you in will not be complete if you are missing. Each person is important and unique. So be committed to the position I have called you to in the body. If you don't know, just ask Me and I will tell you where you need to be placed in the body.

Each piece fits into My plan and you are to have unity in the body. You are all anointed by Me for My purpose and your anointing is just as important as anyone else.

Father, I declare I am unique and You have placed me in the position You have called me to and I will be committed to that position. In Jesus' name Amen.

❖DAY 4❖
Read 1 Corinthians 12:2-27; Romans 12:4-5
Ephesians 4:16

As the human body is a unit with many members, each having its own function, so is My body.

The church is a unified body under the headship of Me, but the members (you) have different functions and should be mutually dependent on one another. You need to encourage one another and be there for one another.

Father, I declare I am part of the body of Christ who is the head. I am to be mutually dependent on others and be an encouragement to others. In Jesus' name Amen.

❖DAY 5❖
Read 1 Corinthians 12:2-27; Romans 12:4-5
Ephesians 4:16

You are held together by My anointing of each joint. Every joint, every part is essential for full growth. There are not any insignificant parts of the body. You are all significant and unique. You need to build each other up and edify one another.

Father, I declare I am held together with the body by Your anointing of each joint. I am essential to the body for full growth. I am significant and unique. I will build each other up and edify others. In Jesus' name Amen.

❖DAY 6❖
Read 1 Corinthians 12:2-27; Romans 12:4-5
Ephesians 4:16

You are closely joined and knit together and grow to maturity by this unity in the body. You are to be joined and knit together like your joints and ligaments are closely joined and knit together in your body. You couldn't function very well without your joints and ligaments, could you?

The unity of My body is very important to function according to My will. I am coming back for My bride (the Church) and you are to be a pure and spotless bride. Unity is part of being pure and spotless.

Father, I declare I am closely joined and knit together in the body of Christ like the joints and ligaments are closely joined and knit together in my body. I couldn't function very well without my joints and ligaments. Neither can Your body function without being closely joined and knit together. In Jesus' name Amen.

Read 1 Corinthians 12:2-27; Romans 12:4-5
Ephesians 4:16

1.   Each part of the body is what?

2.   What does God compare His body to?

3.   What does God assign us to?

4.   What is the Church?

5.   What are you held together by?

6.   How is the body of Christ to be joined and knit together?

NOTES:

WEEK 25
❖GOD IS FOR YOU❖
❧❧❧❧❧❧❧❧❧❧❧

❖DAY 1❖
Read Romans 8:31-39; Psalm 118:6
John 16:33; 1 John 5:4

I know you feel a lot of times that I am against you. Father loved you so much He gave Me up for you, to die for your sins (John 3:16). Don't you think He will give you everything else that you need in life?

We are for you not against you in any way. I came freely to die for you and save you from your sins. I forgave you of all your sins and healed you of all your diseases (Psalm 103:3).

Father, I declare You are for me and not against me in any way. You sent Jesus to die for me and You forgave me of all my sins and healed all my diseases. Thank You Father. In Jesus' name Amen.

❖DAY 2❖
Read Romans 8:31-39; Psalm 118:6
John 16:33; 1 John 5:4

You are in right standing with Me and you are a chosen people, a royal priesthood, a holy nation, and My own possession. I called you out of darkness, into My wonderful light.

No one can accuse you or condemn you for I died for you and was raised to life for you. I am sitting in the place of honor at the right hand of our Father, pleading for you. I intercede for you daily.

Father, I declare I am in right standing with You and I am a chosen people, a royal priesthood, a holy nation, and Your possession. Thank You for calling me out of darkness into Your wonderful light. Thank You no one can accuse me or condemn me because You died for me. In Jesus' name Amen.

❖DAY 3❖
Read Romans 8:31-39; Psalm 118:6
John 16:33; 1 John 5:4

There is nothing that can separate you from My love. Nothing in the universe has the power to diminish My love toward you. Troubles, pressures, and problems are unable to come between you and My love.

In the midst of all these struggles, you triumph over them all, for I have made you more than conquerors and My love is your glorious victory over everything (The Passion Translation).

Father, I declare there is nothing that can separate me from Your love. Nothing in the universe has the power to diminish Your love toward me. No kind of troubles can come between me and Your love. I declare I am more than a conqueror and I triumph over all my struggles because of Your love. In Jesus' name Amen.

❖DAY 4❖
Read Romans 8:31-39; Psalm 118:6
John 16:33; 1 John 5:4

You can live in confidence that there is nothing in the universe with the power to separate you from My love. You can be convinced that My love will triumph over death, life's troubles, depression, fallen angels, and dark rulers in the heavens. There is nothing in your present or future circumstances that can weaken My love.

There is no power above you or beneath you, no power that could ever be found in the universe that can distance you from My passionate love, which I lavish upon you. I love you now and forever (The Passion Translation).

Father, I declare I live in confidence that there is nothing in the universe with the power to separate me from Your love. I am convinced that Your love will triumph over death, life's troubles, and dark rulers in the heavens. Nothing can weaken Your love for me. Thank You that no power can distance me from Your passionate love. In Jesus' name Amen.

❖DAY 5❖
Read Romans 8:31-39; Psalm 118:6
John 16:33; 1 John 5:4

Because of My love for you, you can know that I am for you and you do not have to fear what man can do to you.

I will stand beside you and rescue you. You will triumph over them all (Psalm 118:7 The Passion Translation). I will never leave you or forsake you. I love you.

Thank You, Father, for Your love that lets me know that You are for me and I do not have to fear what man can do to me. You stand beside me and will rescue me. I will triumph over them all. I declare You will never leave me or forsake me because of Your great love. In Jesus' name Amen.

❖DAY 6❖
Read Romans 8:31-39; Psalm 118:6
John 16:33; 1 John 5:4

You will have trouble and sorrows in this world but you can be courageous because I have conquered the world for you. You can have peace which is in you and great confidence as you rest in Me.

You overcome the world because your faith is the victorious power that triumphs over the world. Those who believe in Me as the Son of God are world conquerors, defeating its power.

Father, I declare I will be courageous in troubles because You have conquered the world for me. I have peace and great confidence as I rest in You. My faith in You is the victorious power that causes me to overcome the world, defeating its power. In Jesus' name Amen.

1. How can you know that God is for you and not against you?

2. What is Jesus doing for us at the right hand of the Father?

3. Is there anything that can separate you from God's love?

4. What will triumph over death, life's troubles, depression, fallen angels, and dark rulers in the heavens?

5. Where is God in the midst of your struggles?

6. How can you overcome the world?

NOTES:

WEEK 26
❖COMPLETE IN HIM❖
〜〜〜〜〜〜〜〜〜〜〜

❖DAY 1❖
Read Ephesians 3:14-19; Colossians 2:7
Ephesians 1:23; Colossians 2:9-10

I want to give to you out of My glorious riches, strength, and empowerment in your innermost being by My Spirit. I indwell your innermost being and personality.

By your faith, I will abide and make My permanent home in your heart. May you be rooted deep in My love and founded securely on My love.

Father, I declare You give to me out of Your glorious riches, strength, and empowerment in my innermost being by Your Spirit. You indwell my innermost being and personality. Thank You Lord. In Jesus' name Amen.

❖DAY 2❖
Read Ephesians 3:14-19; Colossians 2:7
Ephesians 1:23; Colossians 2:9-10

When you have your roots deeply planted in Me and become established in your faith, you will be continually built up in Me. You will overflow in your faith with thanksgiving.

Father, I declare because my roots are deeply planted in You and I am established in my faith, I will be continually built up in You. I overflow in my faith with thanksgiving. In Jesus' name Amen.

❖DAY 3❖
Read Ephesians 3:14-19; Colossians 2:7
Ephesians 1:23; Colossians 2:9-10

When you're rooted in Me, you will experience the power to grasp and experience My love, how deeply intimate and far-reaching it is. How enduring and inclusive my love is.

My endless love far surpasses mere knowledge but when you experience My love you will be complete with all the fullness of life and power that comes from Me. You will become a body wholly filled and flooded with Me. I fill everything, everywhere with Myself.

Father, I will experience Your deeply intimate and far-reaching, enduring and all-inclusive love and be complete in You with the fullness of Your life and power. I will become a body wholly filled and flooded with You. In Jesus' name Amen.

❖DAY 4❖
Read Ephesians 3:14-19; Colossians 2:7
Ephesians 1:23; Colossians 2:9-10

Never doubt My mighty power to work in you and accomplish all My love has called you to. I will achieve infinitely more than your greatest request, your most unbelievable dream, and exceed your wildest imagination! I will outdo them all, for My miraculous power constantly energizes you (The Passion Translation).

I am a gentleman and I have made My love, power, and authority and every promise and My presence available to you but if you don't know it's available it will not manifest fully in your life. I am waiting on you to do your part in receiving all I have provided and activate by faith in your life.

Father, I declare I will never doubt Your mighty power to work in me and accomplish all You have called me to. You will achieve infinitely more than my greatest request, my most unbelievable dream, and exceed my wildest imagination. You will outdo them all. Thank You for Your power that constantly energizes me. In Jesus' name Amen.

110

❖DAY 5❖
Read Ephesians 3:14-19; Colossians 2:7
Ephesians 1:23; Colossians 2:9-10

I came to earth in the complete fullness of the Godhead (Father, Son, and Holy Spirit) living in human form.

As you accepted Me as your Lord and Savior, you are complete in Me. You are completely filled with the Godhead (Father, Son, and Holy Spirit) as My fullness overflows within you. Realize the power that is within you and act upon it.

Father, I declare that I am complete in Christ. I am filled with the Godhead (Father, Son, and Holy Spirit) as Your fullness overflows within me. Thank You for the power that is within me. I will act upon it. In Jesus' name Amen.

❖DAY 6❖
Read Ephesians 3:14-19; Colossians 2:7
Ephesians 1:23; Colossians 2:9-10

My glory is in the church because My glory is in you. You are the church which is My body. You are part of My body with a powerful purpose to be achieved through Me and My love.

Through Me give praise to our Father for what has manifested and that will yet be manifested through time and eternity.

Father, I declare Your glory is in the church because Your glory dwells in me. I am part of Your body with a powerful purpose to be achieved through Your love. I give praise and honor to You for what has been manifested and what will yet be manifested through time and eternity. In Jesus' name Amen.

Read Ephesians 3:14-19; Colossians 2:7
Ephesians 1:23; Colossians 2:9-10

1. What does Jesus want to grant us and how is it obtained?

2. How will we be continually built up in Him?

3. What will happen when you experience His love?

4. What will He achieve in and through you?

5. What are you completely filled with?

6. Where is God's glory?

NOTES:

WEEK 27
❖ROYAL PRIESTHOOD❖
ぞぞぞぞぞぞぞぞぞぞぞぞぞ

❖DAY 1❖
Read 1 Peter 1:4-10; Revelation 1:5-6
Psalm 22:3; Exodus 19:5-6; Leviticus 19:2

I am your source of life, a living stone. You will be found stable and secure on this stone. You are like living stones for construction of My vibrant temple, in which you are. My Holy Spirit dwells in you.

Your life is to be holy as I am holy and you will serve as a holy priest offering your life up to Me. You will never regret trusting in Me.

Father, I declare I am like a living stone because I am in You and You are a living stone. I can rest my life on this stone as a foundation. I am holy because You are holy. In Jesus' name Amen.

❖DAY 2❖
Read 1 Peter 2:1-10; Revelation 1:5-6
Psalm 22:3; Exodus 19:5-6; Leviticus 19:2

If you disobey My Word and don't believe it, I am a stone you will trip over, a boulder blocking your way.

If you accepted Me as your Lord and Savior, you are chosen by our Father, chosen for the high calling of priestly work which is to speak out for Me, tell others of the miraculous things done in your life, from being nothing to something, and from being rejected to accepted.

A priest in the Old Testament served in the temple, bringing atonement to the people with sacrifices and worshipping the Father with praises. You are to reign as kings in the earth. That means live your life in abundance.

Father, I declare You have called me for the high calling of priestly work which is speaking out for You, telling others of the miraculous things done in my life, from being nothing to something, and from being rejected to being accepted. I will praise You and give You honor. In Jesus' name Amen.

❖DAY 3❖
Read 1 Peter 2:1-10; Revelation 1:5-6
Psalm 22:3; Exodus 19:5-6; Leviticus 19:2

You are Father's very own possession, chosen by Him, a royal priesthood, holy, and acceptable in His sight. You can show others My goodness because I have called you out of darkness into My marvelous light.

I have made you a kingdom of priests to serve the Father in holiness and righteousness. What is holiness? Being separated to Me. Do not be conformed to this world, but be transformed by the renewing of your mind to My Word (Romans 12:2).

Father, I declare I am Your very own possession, chosen by You, a royal priesthood, holy, and acceptable in Your sight. I will show others Your goodness because You have called me out of darkness into Your marvelous light. In Jesus' name Amen.

❖DAY 4❖
Read 1 Peter 2:1-10; Revelation 1:5-6
Psalm 22:3; Exodus 19:5-6; Leviticus 19:2

To be holy as I am holy you must get rid of all evil behavior. Be done with all deceit, hypocrisy, jealousy, and all unkind speech.

As nursing infants cry out for milk, you must intensely crave the pure spiritual milk of My Word. For My Word will cause you to grow into maturity, fully nourished, and strong for life, especially now that you have had a taste of My goodness and experienced My kindness.

Father, I declare I am done with all deceit, hypocrisy, jealousy, and all unkind speech to be holy as You are holy. I will intensely crave the pure spiritual milk of Your Word, so I can grow into maturity. In Jesus' name Amen.

114

❖DAY 5❖
Read 1 Peter 2:1-10; Revelation 1:5-6
Psalm 22:3; Exodus 19:5-6; Leviticus 19:2

As a royal priesthood you are to praise Me. To thank Me, rejoice over Me as I do you (Zephaniah 3:17), speaking and singing about My glory, virtue, and honor (1 Chronicles 23:30).

Also, praise Me continually on a daily basis (Psalm 145:2). You are to thank Me, bless Me, and bow down before Me. You are the holy one, blessed are You.

Father, I declare I will praise You and rejoice over You, speaking and singing about Your glory, virtue and honor on a daily basis. I will bow down to You and bless You. In Jesus' name Amen.

❖DAY 6❖
Read 1 Peter 2:1-10; Revelation 1:5-6
Psalm 22:3; Exodus 19:5-6; Leviticus 19:2

Praise Me with songs of joy because of My love for you. Enter My gates with thanksgiving and go into My courts with praise because I am good and My love continues forever.

Worship is serving Me as a priest. Praise Me for the glorious grace I have poured out on you and for dying for your sins. I purchased your freedom with My blood on the cross.

Father, I declare I will praise You with songs of joy because of Your love for me. I will enter Your gates with thanksgiving and go into Your courts with praise because You are good and Your love continues forever. I will serve You with my praises and honor You. In Jesus' name Amen.

Read 1 Peter 2:1-10; Revelation 1:5-6
Psalm 22:3; Exodus 19:5-6; Leviticus 19:2

1. What will you never regret doing?

2. What are you chosen for?

3. What can you show others and why?

4. To be holy as He is holy, what must you get rid of?

5. What are you to praise Him for and how often?

6. How are you to enter His gates and His court? What is worship?

NOTES:

WEEK 28
❖GOD'S LOVE IN YOU❖
❧❧❧❧❧❧❧❧❧❧❧❧❧

❖DAY 1❖
Read 1 John 3:14-24; 1 John 4:1-21

I talked a couple times in this book about My love but it is so important for you that I am going to talk about it again this week. You don't realize how much I love you and what that means for your life. I want you to receive such a revelation of My love that it changes you completely.

When you realize how much I love you, you will see yourself differently and see others differently also. You will be able to love others like you never thought you could.

Father, I declare I receive the revelation of Your amazing love for me and I let it change me and change how I see others. In Jesus' name Amen.

❖DAY 2❖
Read 1 John 3:14-24; 1 John 4:1-21

Don't just say you love each other; show the truth by your actions. Your actions will show that you belong to Me. It is a way of life to walk in My love.

When your heart does not condemn you, you can come boldly to Me and speak to Me face to face. Whatever you ask, you shall receive because you keep My Word.

Father, I declare I will show by my actions that I have love for others. I can come boldly to You for my heart does not condemn me and I will receive what I ask. In Jesus' name Amen.

117

❖DAY 3❖
Read 1 John 3:14-24; 1 John 4:1-21

If you obey My Word, your life will be joined in union with Me and I will live and flourish in you. You will know that I live and flourish in you by My Spirit that lives in you.

Don't trust every spirit, but carefully examine what they say to determine if they are of Me, because many false prophets are in the world and they will try to deceive you.

To know who is with My genuine Spirit, they will confess Me as the Christ who has come in the flesh. If he does not acknowledge the truth about Me, that person is not from Me. He has a spirit of Antichrist which is in the world. Be careful!

Father, I declare I obey Your Word so my life will be joined in union with You and You will live and flourish in me. Your Spirit lives in me. I will not trust every spirit but will carefully examine what they say to determine if they are of You. I will not be deceived. In Jesus' name Amen.

❖DAY 4❖
Read 1 John 3:14-24; 1 John 4:1-21

My Spirit that lives in you is greater than the spirit that lives in the world. Through My Spirit you have the victory in your life. Those that know Me will listen to you but those who do not belong to Me, do not listen to you. This is how you can know if someone has My Spirit or the spirit of deception.

You are loved by Me so you are to let My love continually pour from you to one another because I am love. If you love others you are fathered by Me and experience an intimate knowledge of Me. If you don't love others, then you don't know Me because I am love.

Father, I declare Your Spirit lives in me and is greater than the spirit that lives in the world. I am loved by You and I will let Your love continually pour from me to others because You are love. In Jesus' name Amen.

118

❖DAY 5❖
Read 1 John 3:14-24; 1 John 4:1-21

Father showed how much He loved you by sending Me, His Son into the world so that you can have eternal life through Me. This is real love: not that you loved the Father but that He loved you and sent Me as a sacrifice to take away your sins.

Since we loved you that much, you surely ought to love each other. No one has ever seen Me but if you love each other, I live in you and My love is brought to full expression in you.

Father, I declare You showed me how much You loved me by sending Jesus to take away my sins. I will love others because You live in me and Your love lives in me. In Jesus' name Amen.

❖DAY 6❖
Read 1 John 3:14-24; 1 John 4:1-21

I am love and all who live in love live in Me and I live in you. As you live in Me, your love grows more perfect. As I am, so are you in this world.

Do not fear because My perfect love expels all fear. If you are fearful, you have not experienced My perfect love. Love each other because I loved you first.

You cannot say you love Me whom you cannot see, and hate your brother whom you can see. Those who love Me, love others.

Father, I declare You are love and I live in love and You live in me. My love grows more perfect as I live in You. I will not fear because Your perfect love that lives in me expels all fear. I will love others because I love You. In Jesus' name Amen.

119

Read 1 John 3:14-24; 1 John 4:1-21

1. What will you be able to do when you realize how much God loves you?

2. What will your actions show?

3. How will you know who has the Spirit of God in them?

4. Why are you to let God's love pour out from you?

5. How did the Father show how much He loved you?

6. Why should you not fear? Why should you love others? Can you hate your brother and say you love God?

NOTES:

WEEK 29
❖JESUS INTERCEDES FOR YOU❖
‹‹‹‹‹‹‹‹‹‹‹‹‹‹‹‹‹‹‹‹‹

❖DAY 1❖
Read Hebrews 7:25; Hebrews 1:13-2:4
Romans 8:34; Hebrews 9:24

I am a representative for you in heaven. As a man who has walked on the earth, I know what you are going through and can empathize with you. I intercede for you to our Father because I know your weaknesses and I give you strength and support.

Our Father and I sit and have a conversation about you. I tell Him things you need. We have such a great time discussing all the great things in store for you.

Thank You Jesus for representing me in heaven to our Father and empathizing with me. Thank You for pleading my case and giving me strength. In Jesus' name Amen.

❖DAY 2❖
Read Hebrews 7:25; Hebrews 1:13-2:4
Romans 8:34; Hebrews 9:24

As you represent Me on the earth telling others about Me and what I can do for them, I am representing you in heaven, telling our Father about you. I tell the angels to go to your rescue in times of need or encourage you when you are down. They are ministering spirits to serve those who are children of God.

I am ministering in heaven for you as the High Priest in the Old Testament ministered in the temple made by man's hands. They made sacrifices for their sins as well as man's sins and interceded on behalf of the people. They ministered for the people and worshipped our Father.

Jesus, I declare I represent You on the earth telling others about You and what You can do for them. Thank You for representing me in heaven to our Father and ministering for me in heaven. In Jesus' name Amen.

❖DAY 3❖
Read Hebrews 7:25; Hebrews 1:13-2:4
Romans 8:34; Hebrews 9:24

I am now your High Priest in heaven because I came to sacrifice Myself and My blood was shed for you once and for all. I was the final sacrifice.

I now sit at the right hand of our Father ministering and interceding for you and worshipping Him for all the things He has done and is doing for you.

Father, thank You for Jesus the sacrifice on the cross and shed blood for all my sins. Thank You, Jesus, for ministering and interceding for me. In Jesus' name Amen.

❖DAY 4❖
Read Hebrews 7:25; Hebrews 1:13-2:4
Romans 8:34; Hebrews 9:24

The Holy Spirit joins in on our conversations about you. He is given what to say to you to guide you in the right direction and He tells you things to come.

My Holy Spirit dwells in you. You are the temple of My Holy Spirit. Holy Spirit is your advocate who is always with you. He is your intercessor, comforter, helper, and counselor. He guides you into all truth of the Word.

We love you so very much and want the best for you. You need to stay in My Word, praying in tongues, and listen to the leading of My Spirit. You do that and you will have victory in every area of your life.

Father, thank You for the Holy Spirit who dwells in me, who guides me in the way I should go and tells me things to come. Thank You for loving me. In Jesus' name Amen.

❖DAY 5❖
Read Hebrews 7:25; Hebrews 1:13-2:4
Romans 8:34; Hebrews 9:24

When Holy Spirit converses with our Father and Me, He is acting like an attorney who appears in court in another's behalf. He will intercede what is spoken to Me and I will take it to our Father.

We are a three part being Father, Son, and Holy Spirit. We all work together for your benefit.

Father, I declare I am the temple of the Holy Spirit. He is my intercessor, comforter, helper, and counselor. He guides me into all truth. He will intercede what is spoken by me and Jesus pleads my case before You Father. Thank You that all three of You work together for my benefit. In Jesus' name Amen.

❖DAY 6❖
Read Hebrews 7:25; Hebrews 1:13-2:4
Romans 8:34; Hebrews 9:24

I know you are thinking how can I be conversing with our Father about you and all the other Christians in the world all at the same time. Don't forget I am omnipotent which is having unlimited power and able to do anything. I am omniscient which is all knowing, all wise, and all seeing. I am also omnipresent which is infinite and present everywhere at the same time.

So I have no trouble conversing with our Father about you and everyone else at the same time. Just trust Me that nothing is impossible especially where our Father and the Holy Spirit is concerned. We have no trouble knowing you intimately just as a natural father knows his children but we (Father, Son, and Holy Spirit) know all and see all.

Father, I declare You are omnipotent, omniscient, and omnipresent. You are able to converse with Father God about me and every other Christian in the world at the same time. Thank You for being intimately involved with me. In Jesus' name Amen.

123

❖DAY 7-SUMMARY QUESTIONS❖
Read Hebrews 7:25; Hebrews 1:13-2:4;
Romans 8:34; Hebrews 9:24

1. What is Jesus doing in heaven with the Father?

2. Jesus is ministering in heaven as our what?

3. Where is Jesus sitting in heaven and doing what?

4. Who joins in the conversation with Jesus and the Father?

5. What does the Holy Spirit act as when He converses with Jesus and the Father?

6. What three things is Jesus to you? What does it give Him the ability to do?

NOTES:

WEEK 30
❖NO CONDEMNATION IN CHRIST❖
❧❧❧❧❧❧❧❧❧❧❧❧❧❧❧❧❧❧

❖DAY 1❖
Read Romans 5:18; 8:1, 34; John 3:18
John 5:24; Romans 14:12-13

Adam's one sin brings condemnation to everyone. When you were born, you were born into Adam's sin but My one act of righteousness brings a right relationship with Me and new life for everyone.

When you accepted Me as your Lord and Savior, you were born again and free from condemnation.

Father, I declare I have accepted You as my Lord and Savior so I am in right relationship with You and free from condemnation. In Jesus' name Amen.

❖DAY 2❖
Read Romans 5:18; 8:1, 34; John 3:18
John 5:24; Romans 14:12-13

Condemnation means judgment and blame. I do not judge you or blame you for anything as long as you are in Me. My life-giving Spirit frees you from the power of sin that leads to death and judgment.

Who will condemn you? No one will condemn you. No one is to condemn you and you are not to condemn or judge others. Judge not or you will be judged. Love one another as I have loved you.

Father, I declare I am not judged or condemned and I am not to judge or condemn others. In Jesus' name Amen.

❖DAY 3❖
Read Romans 5:18; 8:1, 34; John 3:18
John 5:24; Romans 14:12-13

Since you accepted Me as your Lord and Savior there is no longer any condemnation for you because you believe in Me, but the unbeliever already lives under condemnation because they do not believe in My name. Here is the basis for their judgment, My Light has now come into the world, but the hearts of people love their darkness more than My Light, because they want the darkness to conceal their evil.

So the wicked hate My Light and try to hide from it, for their lives are fully exposed in My Light. But those who love My truth will come out into My Light and welcome its exposure, for My Light will reveal that their fruitful works were produced by Me. (John 3:18-21 The Passion Translation).

Father, I declare there is no longer any condemnation for me because I believe in Jesus as my Lord and Savior. I welcome the Light in my life to expose that my fruitful works were produced by You. In Jesus' name Amen.

❖DAY 4❖
Read Romans 5:18; 8:1, 34; John 3:18
John 5:24; Romans 14:12-13

I speak an eternal truth; you will never face condemnation for in Me you have passed from death into the realm of eternal life.

At this moment, you are living in eternal life. It doesn't start when you get to heaven; it started when you accepted Me as your Lord and Savior because I am eternal life and I am in you.

Father, I declare I will never face condemnation because in You I have passed from death into the realm of eternal life. Thank You Lord. In Jesus' name Amen.

❖DAY 5❖
Read Romans 5:18; 8:1, 34; John 3:18
John 5:24; Romans 14:12-13

You will give an account to our Father, but you are not condemned. You need to stop condemning one another. Even though you don't speak your judgment, thinking it is just as bad.

Just because others are not like you, you have no right to judge or condemn others. Pray for them instead of passing judgment on them. Treat others the way you want to be treated. Wouldn't you rather someone pray for you rather than judge you? I'm sure you would, so pray for one another. No one is without sin. No one is perfect.

Just like the woman caught in adultery, I said to those who were condemning her that the one without sin was to throw the first stone. They walked away. They could not condemn her nor could I (John 8:4-11).

Father, I declare I will not condemn others in speech or in thought because I have no right to condemn another because I have sinned also. I am not perfect. I will pray for others. In Jesus' name Amen.

❖DAY 6❖
Read Romans 5:18; 8:1, 34; John 3:18
John 5:24; Romans 14:12-13

You are to live in such a way that you will not cause another believer to stumble and fall.

Just as I said to Peter to get behind Me when he was saying that I was not going to die. I said he was a dangerous trap to Me. He was trying to convince Me to do other than what God has sent Me to do. He was seeing things from a human point of view, not from God's.

Seek Me before you speak and condemn another person. I will take care of the situation.

Father, I declare I will live in such a way that I will not cause another believer to stumble or fall. I will seek You before I judge or condemn another. In Jesus' name Amen.

Read Romans 5:18; 8:1, 34; John 3:18
John 5:24; Romans 14:12-13

1. What brings a right relationship with God?

2. Who will condemn you?

3. Who is under condemnation?

4. What are you living in as a believer?

5. What are you to do rather than condemn someone?

6. How are you to live toward others?

NOTES:

WEEK 31
❖OVERCOMERS IN CHRIST❖
❧❧❧❧❧❧❧❧❧❧❧❧❧❧

❖DAY 1❖
Read Revelation 12:10-11; Leviticus 17:11
1 John 4:4; John 16:33; 1 John 5:4-5

The devil is out to get you. He roams about like a roaring lion, looking for someone to devour (1 Peter 5:8).

The only power the devil has is the power you give to him. If you submit to Me, resist the devil and he will flee from you (James 4:7). He comes to steal, kill, and destroy. I have come to give you an abundant life.

Father, I declare I will submit to You and resist the devil and he will flee from me. Thank You for giving me an abundant and victorious life. In Jesus' name Amen.

❖DAY 2❖
Read Revelation 12:10-11; Leviticus 17:11
1 John 4:4; John 16:33; 1 John 5:4-5

How do you overcome and resist the devil? You overcome by My blood and the word of your testimony. The life of the flesh is in the blood.

Life and blood were given upon the altar for the specific purpose of making atonement, or attaining reconciliation with Father God in the Old Testament. Apart from the shedding of blood or giving a life, there was no atonement.

This established ordinance is reaffirmed in the New Covenant in Hebrew 9:22 which states, "Without the shedding of blood, there is no forgiveness". The New Covenant in My shed blood fulfilled the requirements of the Old Covenant for redemption.

Thank You, Father, for the shed blood of Jesus on the cross for my forgiveness and redemption. In Jesus' name Amen.

❖DAY 3❖
Read Revelation 12:10-11; Leviticus 17:11
1 John 4:4; John 16:33; 1 John 5:4-5

With My shed blood on the cross, you can overcome. My blood gives you the victory in life and also gives you authority in Me to resist the devil. He will flee from you when you resist him.

I am in you and I am greater than the devil. Get this revelation that I am in you and greater than the devil who is in the world, confess it and you will overcome.

Father, I declare I can overcome and have victory over the devil by the shed blood of Jesus that gives me the authority over the devil. In Jesus' name Amen.

❖DAY 4❖
Read Revelation 12:10-11; Leviticus 17:11
1 John 4:4; John 16:33; 1 John 5:4-5

You also defeat the devil by the word of your testimony. Your testimony is speaking the Word of truth which is My Word and what your relationship with Me has given you in life.

Declare your faith in My accomplished work of the cross and constantly participate in My ultimate victory, overcoming the devil by My power of the cross and your testimony of faith being firmly fixed in My triumph.

Father, I declare I will overcome the devil by the blood of the lamb which is Jesus and by the word of my testimony. I will speak the Word of truth and of Your love for me. In Jesus' name Amen.

❖DAY 5❖
Read Revelation 12:10-11; Leviticus 17:11
1 John 4:4; John 16:33; 1 John 5:4-5

In this world, you will have trials and tribulations, but you can have peace and victory because I have overcome the world. I know you wonder how I can say that I have overcome the world, but through Me and My shed blood on the cross, the devil is defeated.

You are asking, "If that is the case, how come I feel defeated and everything is going wrong?" I didn't say you wouldn't be tempted or harassed by the devil, I said you would have victory and be an overcomer. I am with you through every trial you face. You are more than a conqueror through Me.

You must know what My Word says to defeat the devil. As I did in the desert when I was tempted, I said, "It is written" to the devil and he had to flee. I give you the authority in My name to use My Word and rebuke him.

Father, I declare even in the midst of trials and tribulation I will have peace and victory because You have overcome the world by Your shed blood on the cross and Your resurrection. Thank You. In Jesus' name Amen.

❖DAY 6❖
Read Revelation 12:10-11; Leviticus 17:11
1 John 4:4; John 16:33; 1 John 5:4-5

You can also achieve victory in your life and be an overcomer by your faith in Me that I am the Son of God. You must have faith and not doubt to be an overcomer.

To be an overcomer, you must have faith in My shed blood on the cross, believe in the word of your testimony, realize that I have overcome the world, and I am with you in and through every trial.

Father, I declare I have faith to achieve this victory over the world and the devil by believing Jesus is the Son of God, by Your shed blood on the cross, by the word of my testimony, and that You have overcome this world. I have authority in Your name to use Your Word against the devil. In Jesus' name Amen.

Read Revelation 12:10-11; Leviticus 17:11
1 John 4:4; John 16:33; 1 John 5:4-5

1. What do you need to do to have the devil flee from you?

2. What fulfilled the requirements of the Old Covenant for redemption?

3. Who is in you and greater than the devil?

4. What is your testimony of?

5. What must you know to defeat the devil?

6. What are the four things talked about this week to be an overcomer?

NOTES:

WEEK 32
❖MEASURE OF FAITH❖
~~~~~~~~~~~~~~~~

❖DAY 1❖
Read Romans 12:1-3; Hebrews 12:1-3
Hebrews 11:1-6; Mark 11:22-24; Romans 10:17

Our Father has given you a measure of faith. It's not the faith of a mustard seed but the faith that created the heavens and the earth. The faith that raised Me up from the grave.

This faith is in you. When you were born again into our family, you received this faith. It permeates through you and is what will help you to overcome in this world.

Father, I declare I have a measure of faith. It is the faith that created the heavens and the earth and the faith that raised Jesus from the dead. Through my faith, I will overcome this world. In Jesus' name Amen.

❖DAY 2❖
Read Romans 12:1-3; Hebrews 12:1-3
Hebrews 11:1-6; Mark 11:22-24; Romans 10:17

You think that some people were given more faith because they seem so strong in their faith and seem to never falter. Their faith is stronger because they are in My Word and grow their faith by reading, confessing, and meditating on My Word.

Study and meditate on My Word and you will increase your faith and it will be strong enough to stand firm in the midst of trials and tribulations.

Father, I declare You have given everyone the same measure of faith when we were born again. I can grow and strengthen my faith by studying and meditating on Your Word and confessing it. In Jesus' name Amen.

❖DAY 3❖
Read Romans 12:1-3; Hebrews 12:1-3
Hebrews 11:1-6; Mark 11:22-24; Romans 10:17

I am the developer and finisher of your faith. You must keep your eyes focused on Me just as the runner must keep his focus on the finish line to get his reward.

I endured the cross to give you the faith to stand firm in this life. You just need to put the Word first, meditate on My Word, and then act on My Word. This puts faith on the line. Faith begins to grow when My Word becomes a vital part of your daily conduct and daily speech. By doing this, you will have victory in your life.

Father, I declare you are the developer and finisher of my faith as I stay focused on Jesus. My faith will grow as I put Your Word first, meditate on Your Word, and act on Your Word. In Jesus' name Amen.

❖DAY 4❖
Read Romans 12:1-3; Hebrews 12:1-3
Hebrews 11:1-6; Mark 11:22-24; Romans 10:17

What is faith? Faith is the heavenly substance of what you desire in your heart. Faith is NOW. Hope is in the future. Faith calls things that be not as though they were (Romans 4:16-25).

What do I mean by this? If you are sick, faith speaks My Word. It speaks of health and healing, not speaking what you have. Don't deny that you are sick but speak what you desire instead of talking about your sickness. It is impossible to please Me without faith. It is impossible to receive My promises without faith. Walk in faith and do not doubt.

Father, I declare that faith is NOW. I will call things that are not as though they were. I will please You by walking in faith and not doubt. In Jesus' name Amen.

134

❖DAY 5❖
Read Romans 12:1-3; Hebrews 12:1-3
Hebrews 11:1-6; Mark 11:22-24; Romans 10:17

You are free to use My faith. My Word says "Whosoever". You are a whosoever so you can use My faith. My faith is My gift to you (Ephesians 2:8).

You can speak to your mountain and it shall be cast into the sea. If you believe the things that you say and do not doubt, you shall have whatsoever you say. That includes negative things as well as positive things. That is why you need to put My Word first, make it final authority, meditate on My Word, act on My Word, and pray in My Spirit.

Father, I declare I am free to use Your faith. I can speak to my mountain and it will be removed and cast into the sea. If I believe and do not doubt, I can have whatever I say. I will speak Your Word instead of my mountain. In Jesus' name Amen.

❖DAY 6❖
Read Romans 12:1-3; Hebrews 12:1-3
Hebrews 11:1-6; Mark 11:22-24; Romans 10:17

How does faith come? It comes by hearing and hearing My Word. When you hear My Word, you will receive truth and the truth you hear will set you free.

There are several different ways to hear My Word. Listen to different preachers preach My Word. Read My Word out loud, confess My Word over your situations. Meditate on My Word, muttering to yourself My truths. When you hear the Word over and over, you will begin to increase your faith and be victorious and an overcomer in this life.

Father, I declare that I will hear Your Word by listening to preachers preach, confessing Your Word over my situations, reading Your Word out loud, and meditating on Your Word. I will increase in my faith when I do this and be an overcomer in this life. In Jesus' name Amen.

Read Romans 12:1-3; Hebrews 12:1-3
Hebrews 11:1-6; Mark 11:22-24; Romans 10:17

1. What kind of faith did our Father God give to us?

2. Why are some people stronger in their faith?

3. Faith begins to grow when you do what?

4. What is faith?

5. How can you have what you say?

6. How does faith come to you?

NOTES:

WEEK 33
❖HOPE IN CHRIST❖
~~~~~~~~~~~

❖DAY 1❖
Read 1 Thessalonians 1:3; 5:8; Romans 5:1-5
I Corinthians 13:13; Colossians 1:4-5; Romans 15:13

In Me you have faith, love, and enduring hope. Last week, I talked about faith. Hope, love, and faith go together. Hope is confident expectation based on solid certainty. Your hope rests on My promises.

Hope is never inferior to faith, but is an extension of faith. Faith is NOW; hope is confidence in the future. Faith is the substance of things hoped for, the evidence of things not see (Hebrews 11:1).

Father, I declare I have faith, love, and hope in You. I have enduring hope in things to come in You. In Jesus' name Amen.

❖DAY 2❖
Read 1 Thessalonians 1:3; 5:8; Romans 5:1-5
I Corinthians 13:13; Colossians 1:4-5; Romans 15:13

Since you belong to the day, which means to the light or to Me, you must stay alert and clearheaded. What are you to be aware of? You are to be alert and aware of the evil around you and the devil roaming around as a roaring lion to devour you.

You are to be alert and clearheaded by placing the breastplate of faith and love over your heart. This breastplate is different than the breastplate of righteousness in Ephesians 6:10-18. You must walk in faith to please Me and you must walk in love because I am love.

You also must have a helmet of the hope of salvation which is deliverance from evil and it will save you from now until I return for you. Be confident in your salvation in Me.

Father, I declare I belong to You and I will stay alert and clearheaded of the evil around me and the devil roaming around waiting to devour me. I put on the breastplate of faith and love and the helmet of the hope of salvation which will save me from now until You return for me. In Jesus' name Amen.

❖DAY 3❖
Read 1 Thessalonians 1:3; 5:8; Romans 5:1-5
I Corinthians 13:13; Colossians 1:4-5; Romans 15:13

Your faith in Me transfers My righteousness to you and our Father declares you righteous in His eyes. You can enjoy true and lasting peace with our Father because of what I have done on the cross. You can rejoice in the hope of My glory.

Even when you experience times of trouble and pressure you can have hope and joyful confidence, knowing that these troubles will develop in you patient endurance. And patient endurance will refine your character and a refined character leads you back to hope.

This hope is not disappointing because you can now experience My endless love cascading into your heart through My Holy Spirit who lives in you.

Father, I declare I am righteous in Your eyes because of Jesus' death on the cross. I will enjoy lasting peace because of Jesus. I can rejoice in the hope of Your glory. Troubles will produce patient endurance, patient endurance will refine my character and a refined character will bring me back to hope. Thank You for Your endless love cascading into my heart through the Holy Spirit. In Jesus' name Amen.

❖DAY 4❖
Read 1 Thessalonians 1:3; 5:8; Romans 5:1-5
I Corinthians 13:13; Colossians 1:4-5; Romans 15:13

1 Corinthians 13 states that knowledge will pass away and tongues will cease when the perfect comes which means when I return for you but faith, hope, and love will remain. Love surpasses them all. I am love and I dwell in you.

Your understanding is incomplete now but when I return you will understand everything. Let your hope remain in what is to come.

Father, I declare knowledge and tongues will pass away when You return for me. Faith, hope, and love will remain but love surpasses them all because You are love and You dwell in me. I look forward to understanding everything when You return for me. In Jesus' name Amen.

❖DAY 5❖
Read 1 Thessalonians 1:3; 5:8; Romans 5:1-5
I Corinthians 13:13; Colossians 1:4-5; Romans 15:13

Faith, hope, and love are genuine qualities of the Colossian church. They are qualities you must strive for. You must have faith, for without faith you cannot please Me. You must have love, for without love you have nothing. You must have hope for without hope, faith and love cannot manifest.

As stated before, these three go together but love is the greatest. I am love and I dwell within you and you must understand how much I love you to receive this revelation. Pursue My faith, love, and hope.

Father, I declare I have the qualities of faith, love, and hope that the Colossian church had. I will pursue Your faith, love, and hope. In Jesus' name Amen.

❖DAY 6❖
Read 1 Thessalonians 1:3; 5:8; Romans 5:1-5
I Corinthians 13:13; Colossians 1:4-5; Romans 15:13

My Holy Spirit imparts not only spiritual gifts to you, but also joy and peace and hope. You can rejoice in hope and abound which means to have a great surplus of hope that My Holy Spirit gives you (Romans 14:17).

The power or energy, strength, and might of My Holy Spirit give you these great qualities. Walk in them and you will be an overcomer.

Father, I declare that the mighty, powerful Holy Spirit gives me joy, peace, and hope. I can rejoice and I do abound in hope which is solid confidence in You. In Jesus' name Amen.

Read 1 Thessalonians 1:3; 5:8; Romans 5:1-5
I Corinthians 13:13; Colossians 1:4-5; Romans 15:13

1. In Jesus what do you have?

2. What are you to be aware of and alert to? How are you to be alert and clearheaded?

3. What will your troubles develop? When troubles come and develop you, how can you know you will not be disappointed in hope?

4. What surpasses faith and hope?

5. What qualities must you strive for?

6. What does the Holy Spirit impart to you?

NOTES:

WEEK 34
❖NAME WRITTEN IN BOOK OF LIFE❖

❖DAY 1❖
Read Luke 10:17-20; Philippians 4:3
Revelation 3:5; 20:12-15; 21:27

I sent out the seventy-two disciples to heal the sick and preach the message of salvation. When they returned they were excited about the fact that even the demons obeyed them in My name.

I told them I had seen Satan fall from heaven like lightning when they ministered and they had authority over them but their source of joy shouldn't be that these spirits submit to their authority, but that their names are written in the Book of Life in heaven. I say the same to you. Rejoice that your name is written in the Book of Life.

Father, I declare the demons obey me in Jesus' name, but I will rejoice more in the fact that my name is written in the Book of Life that is in heaven. Thank You Lord. In Jesus' name Amen.

❖DAY 2❖
Read Luke 10:17-20; Philippians 4:3
Revelation 3:5; 20:12-15; 21:27

What is this Book of Life that your name is written in? When you accepted Me as your Lord and Savior, our Father wrote your name in the Book of Life which will be opened at the time of judgment. If your name is not in the book, you will be cast into hell with all the demons.

I know you think that our Father would not send anyone to hell and he won't. If your name is not written in the book, it is your choice to not receive Me into your life. Once your name is written in this book, it will not be blotted out. So make sure your name is written in this book by accepting Me as your Lord and Savior. That is the only way.

Thank You, Father, for sending Jesus to die for my sins and for rising from the dead that I may live. Forgive me of all my sins. I accept Jesus as my Lord and Savior and ask that my name be written in the Book of Life. In Jesus' name Amen.

141

❖DAY 3❖
Read Luke 10:17-20; Philippians 4:3
Revelation 20:12-15; 3:5; 21:27

In heaven, you will experience victory and be dressed in white robes. I will never, no never erase your name from the Book of Life. I will acknowledge your name before our Father and His angels.

I saw you before you were born. Every day of your life was recorded in My book. Every moment was laid out before a single day had passed (Psalms 139:16 New Living Translation). This is a different book than the Book of Life.

Father, I declare I will experience victory and be dressed in white robes. My name will never be erased from the Book of Life. I ask You to show me what is written in this book of my life You have written before I was born. In Jesus' name Amen.

❖DAY 4❖
Read Luke 10:17-20; Philippians 4:3
Revelation 20:12-15; 3:5; 21:27

All of Psalm 139 is talking about how I have examined your heart and know everything about you. I know your thoughts and where you are at. You can't hide from Me.

I made you and knit you together in your mother's womb. I saw you as you were being formed into a wonderfully, complex, and marvelous person. I am always with you and will guide you. I think precious thoughts of you. Don't ever doubt My love.

What does this have to do with the Book of Life? I just want you to know how much I love and care for you. I want you to know the importance of your name being in the Book of Life.

Thank You, Father, for knowing everything about me and forming me into a wonderful, complex, and marvelous person. I declare You love me more than I can ever understand. Thank You. In Jesus' name Amen.

❖DAY 5❖
Read Luke 10:17-20; Philippians 4:3
Revelation 20:12-15; 3:5; 21:27

Your name being written in the Book of Life causes you to be a citizen of heaven. You are no longer part of this world but seated in heavenly places with Me. You live in this world, but you are not to be a part of it. You are a member of the family of God.

You are the temple of My Holy Spirit (1 Corinthians 3:16; 6:19). My Spirit lives in you. You do not belong to yourself if you accepted Me as Your Lord and Savior, you were bought with a price by My blood shed on the cross. You are holy because I am holy and you are My temple.

Father, I declare I am a citizen of heaven. I am no longer a part of this world. I live in this world but I am not to be a part of it. I am a member of Your family. You are my Father and I am a joint heir of Jesus Christ. I am the temple of the Holy Spirit and I am holy because You are holy and dwell in me. In Jesus' name Amen.

❖DAY 6❖
Read Luke 10:17-20; Philippians 4:3
Revelation 20:12-15; 3:5; 21:27

By having your name written in the Book of Life, you have a lot of benefits and promises. Some will be given in heaven when I return for you, but many you can have and already have while on the earth.

You have everything that I have and that I had on the earth (2 Peter 1:3). You need to learn how to release things from the spiritual realm into the natural. For example, I have provided healing on the cross. It is in you now but you must meditate on My Word and realize you are healed and learn how to release it into the natural. Faith is released where the will of God is known.

Father, I declare I have all that Jesus has in me and I will meditate on Your Word and realize that my faith is released when the will of God is known. In Jesus' name Amen.

Read Luke 10:17-20; Philippians 4:3
Revelation 20:12-15; 3:5; 21:27

1. What should our source of joy be?

2. What is the Book of Life?

3. Is the book God wrote about our life the same as the Book of Life?

4. How important is the Book of Life?

5. What else does the Book of Life cause us to be?

6. How do we get these benefits and promises to manifest in our life?

NOTES:

WEEK 35
❖HOLY SPIRIT AND HIS ANOINTING❖

❖DAY 1❖
Read 1 Corinthians 3:16-17; John 14:16-18
John 16:8-13; Acts 10:38

I want to introduce you to My Holy Spirit. You may think you know Him, but is He a reality in your life? You may have been baptized in the Holy Spirit and you may speak with tongues. He is more than just a force or an influence in your life. He is not an "it". Holy Spirit is a person with a personality. He is God-an equal member of the three-person Godhead, Father, Son (Myself), and Holy Spirit.

Holy Spirit didn't just come into being when He was sent to the earth to empower believers, He goes all the way back to the beginning (Genesis 1:2).

Father, Thank You for Holy Spirit. I want Him to be a reality in my life not just a force or influence in my life. I want to know Him and be led by Him. In Jesus' name Amen.

❖DAY 2❖
Read 1 Corinthians 3:16-17; John 14:16-18
John 16:8-13; Acts 10:38

This person dwells within you. You are the temple of My Holy Spirit. How did My Spirit come to live in you? Whenever you accepted Me as your Lord and Savior, My Holy Spirit came to live in you. He indwells your innermost being and personality and causes you to be holy because He is holy (Ephesians 3:16).

Father, I declare I am the temple of the Holy Spirit. When I accepted Jesus as Lord and Savior, He came to live in my spirit. In Jesus' name Amen.

❖DAY 3❖
Read 1 Corinthians 3:16-17; John 14:16-18
John 16:8-13; Acts 10:38

You are a carrier of My Holy Spirit who is your Comforter, Counselor, Helper, Intercessor, Advocate, Strengthener, and Standby.

He is all these and more. He is all that I was on the earth. He wants you to experience the reality of His presence.

He is present and yearns to participate in your life. He is your friend. He is the Spirit of truth and will guide you in all truth and tell you things to come in the future. He speaks only what He hears from our Father.

Holy Spirit is the one on earth now working in you and through you to glorify our Father. You pray to our Father in My name, by the Holy Spirit. Father wants you to be more aware of the workings of My Holy Spirit in and through you.

Father, I declare Holy Spirit is my Comforter, Counselor, Helper, Intercessor, Advocate, Strengthener, Standby, and Spirit of truth. He is all I need. He is my friend. In Jesus' name Amen.

❖DAY 4❖
Read 1 Corinthians 3:16-17; John 14:16-18
John 16:8-13; Acts 10:38

In John 20:22, I breathed on the disciples and said receive the Holy Spirit. This was after My death and resurrection and was when the disciples were born again. This is what happens when you accept Me as Your Lord and Savior.

In Acts 1:8, I told the disciples they would receive power when the Holy Spirit came upon them and they would be witnesses to Me. On the day of Pentecost in Acts 2:4, they received power and anointing when My Holy Spirit came upon them and Holy Spirit empowered them to pray in tongues. This is a separate experience from salvation.

Father, I declare I have received the power of the Holy Spirit and the Holy Spirit has come upon me. I have been baptized in the Holy Spirit with evidence of speaking in tongues. In Jesus' name Amen.

❖DAY 5❖
Read 1 Corinthians 3:16-17; John 14:16-18
John 16:8-13; Acts 10:38

When My Holy Spirit is a reality in your life, He provides a way through which the anointing, the power can flow. You cannot know the power of My anointing until you experience My presence. My presence isn't some goose bump experience or just feelings that are short lived. It is much more than that. In My presence, you will be transformed, feeling such peace and love, and feeling a mighty rushing river flowing through you.

You must abandon yourself, die to your flesh, empty yourself to be filled with My presence. When you are in My presence, My power can be poured out on you and through you.

Father, I declare the Holy Spirit is a reality in my life. I declare I empty myself, abandon myself, and die to my flesh, so Your presence can fill me. Your power can then be poured out of me. In Jesus' name Amen.

❖DAY 6❖
Read 1 Corinthians 3:16-17; John 14:16-18
John 16:8-13; Acts 10:38

You have an anointing from Me, you have been set apart, specially gifted and prepared by My Holy Spirit and you know the truth because My Spirit teaches you, illuminates your mind, and guards you from error (1 John 2:20 Amp).

My anointing is a must in your life if you want to be used by Me. This anointing comes through obedience. Also, the knowledge of My Word is key to this obedience.

The more you know about Me, the more I can trust you with the power. It will not flow if you are in fear. Boldness is a must. You must have My presence to have the anointing. They work together. Don't miss opportunities that I give you.

Father, I declare I have an anointing from You. I have been set apart, gifted, and prepared by the Holy Spirit and I know Your truth. I declare I am obedient to You and study Your Word to know You. You can trust me with Your power. In Jesus' name Amen.

Read 1 Corinthians 3:16-17; John 14:16-18
John 16:8-13; Acts 10:38

1. Who is Holy Spirit?

2. Where does Holy Spirit live?

3. What does Holy Spirit do for you?

4. Explain the difference between the disciples receiving Holy Spirit at time of salvation and at the time of Pentecost?

5. How can you know the power of Jesus' anointing? What must you do to be filled with His presence?

6. How does His anointing come?

NOTES:

WEEK 36
❖POWER AT PENTECOST❖
 celecelecelecelecelecelecele

❖DAY 1❖
Read Acts 2:1-4; Matthew 3:11

I told the disciples to go to Jerusalem for the promise of power from on high. They were waiting about ten days after I told them to go to Jerusalem and wait for the promise.

They didn't know what to expect but they went and waited and were in total unity together.

Father, thank You for filling me with the Holy Spirit with the evidence of speaking in tongues which gives me the power to fulfill the mission You have called me to. In Jesus' name Amen.

❖DAY 2❖
Read Acts 2:1-4; Matthew 3:11

Some believe that when you accept Me as your Lord and Savior, you receive My Holy Spirit and you do. The filling or baptism of My Spirit is a different experience. I breathed on them and said, "Receive My Holy Spirit" (John 20:22). This is when they were born again and what happens when you accept Me. The disciples were not born again until after I was crucified and rose from the grave and ascended to the Father.

On Pentecost, the work of My Spirit as the Spirit of power (Isaiah 11:2, "might") is to enable the disciples for ministry, witness and service, and to fulfill their mission to the world. They are two separate events.

Thank You, Father, for saving me from my sins and filling me with the Holy Spirit with the evidence of speaking in tongues. In Jesus' name Amen.

Read Acts 2:1-4; Matthew 3:11

Verse 4 of Acts 2 is the initial fulfillment of My promise in Acts 1:5 which says "for John truly baptized with water, but you shall be baptized with My Holy Spirit not many days from now".

So, the disciples went to Jerusalem and they were all together. They didn't know what to expect but when it came, they would know. Some believer's think they have to wait around to receive, but at Pentecost it was given and you only need to ask and I will fill you. My Spirit isn't going to speak for you. You have to start praising Me and I will give you utterance and enable you to speak in tongues.

Father, I declare I am filled with the Holy Spirit with evidence of speaking in tongues. In Jesus' name Amen.

❖DAY 4❖
Read Acts 2:1-4; Matthew 3:11

As they were waiting, suddenly there came a sound as of a rushing mighty wind and it filled the whole house which is the mighty but unseen power of My Holy Spirit (John 3:8). The sound brought the people out to find out what was going on.

What looked like tongues of fire appeared and settled on each one of them, which is a fulfillment of what John the Baptist in Matthew 3:11-12 foretold how My Spirit baptism would be accompanied by wind and fire.

Father, You do things suddenly sometimes so let me be prepared and focused on You so I can receive Your "suddenlies". In Jesus' name Amen.

❖DAY 5❖
Read Acts 2:1-4; Matthew 3:11

To experience My Holy Spirit fullness you must come to Me. When you come to Me, I will save you, then want to fill you continually, pouring My Holy Spirit upon you, enabling you to declare and demonstrate My living power wherever you go until I come again (Ephesians 5:18).

Father, I come to You and ask You to baptize me with the Holy Spirit continually and give me the utterance of speaking in tongues. In Jesus' name Amen.

❖DAY 6❖
Read Acts 2:1-4; Matthew 3:11

They were all filled (diffused throughout their souls) with My Holy Spirit and began to speak in other (different, foreign) languages (tongues). This was the beginning of the Church and I intended it for all generations.

You don't have to be fearful of speaking in tongues. Some say, "I want to know what I am saying?" It involves faith in Me. I will give you the interpretation if you ask Me.

The devil wants you to be fearful because he knows when you pray in tongues, you are speaking directly to My Holy Spirit and he doesn't know what you are saying. Trust Me and be filled.

Father, I declare that I am diffused throughout my soul with the Holy Spirit and will speak in tongues as You give me the utterance. In Jesus' name Amen.

DAY 7 – SUMMARY QUESTIONS
Read Acts 2:1-4; Matthew 3:11

1. What did God tell the disciples to do?

2. What did My Spirit enable the disciples to do on the day of Pentecost?

3. What do you need to do to receive the Holy Spirit with evidence of speaking in tongues?

4. What was the fulfillment of what John the Baptist in Matthew 3:11-12 foretold of the Holy Spirit?

5. What must you do to experience the Holy Spirit?

6. When you speak in tongues, who are you speaking to?

NOTES:

WEEK 37
❖PRIVATE VS. PUBLIC TONGUES❖

~~~~~~~~~~~~~~~~~~~~~~~~~~

❖DAY1❖
Read 1 Corinthians 14:1-5; Jude 1:20
John 14-16

When you are speaking in an unknown tongue, you are not speaking to men but to Me. It is the perfect prayer and only I know what you are saying unless you ask Me for the interpretation and I will give it to you.

The purpose of praying in tongues is for you to be empowered in ministry that is above the limits of human ability and deeper intimacy for fellowship with Me. The language of worship, intercession, personal edification, and revelation from Me are benefits for you when you regularly involve yourself with My Holy Spirit-enabled language as a vital part of your devotional life with Me.

It doesn't give you a superior relationship with Me by praying in tongues. You are no better than the person who does not pray in tongues.

Father, I declare as I pray in the Spirit I will edify myself and receive revelation from You. In Jesus' name Amen.

❖DAY 2❖
Read 1 Corinthians 14:1-5; Jude 1:20
John 14-16

A person who speaks in tongues is strengthened personally, but one who speaks a word of prophecy strengthens the entire church. Speaking in tongues in a church service must have an interpretation. It is a gift of My Spirit (1 Corinthians 12:10). I want to stress the importance of praying in My Spirit in your prayer and devotional times, not the public tongues and interpretation.

Father, I declare as I pray in the Spirit I edify and strengthen myself and receive revelation from You Lord. In Jesus' name Amen.

153

❖DAY 3❖
Read 1 Corinthians 14:1-5; Jude 1:20
John 14-16

Praying in My Spirit is your spirit praying to My Spirit. There may be times My Spirit will encourage you to pray for a certain thing or person but you don't know what to pray. Pray in My Spirit and My Spirit knows what is needed as you pray in tongues (Romans 8:26).

My Spirit does not pray instead of you, but My Spirit takes part with you and makes your weak prayers effective. My Spirit intercedes on your behalf before the throne of our Father God (1 John 2:1).

Father, I declare I am available to You to intercede for whoever or whatever You place in my spirit. Your Spirit will cause my prayers to be effective. In Jesus' name Amen.

❖DAY 4❖
Read 1 Corinthians 14:1-5; Jude 1:20
John 14-16

As you pray in tongues, My Spirit will reveal mysteries and secrets. I will tell you things to come and guide you into all truth (John 16:13).

You seem to have trouble staying focused on Me and are unable to pray in My Spirit very long. Set your mind on things above and praying in My Spirit will become more important to you as you keep your mind set on heavenly things.

Let your spirit dominate your flesh instead of your flesh dominating you. Don't listen to the devil's lies. I like it when you pray in tongues. It is My language. You may not always know what you are praying but I know what you are praying.

Praying in tongues edifies you and gives you strength and revelation from Me. Get into the habit of praying in tongues, it will start flowing easier for you. You lose out on My power and revelation and My presence because you don't pray in the Spirit enough.

Father, I declare You tell me things to come and guide me into all truth and give me revelation of Your Word. In Jesus' name Amen.

❖DAY 5❖
Read 1 Corinthians 14:1-5; Jude 1:20
John 14-16

I asked our Father that He would give you another Comforter (Counselor, Helper, Intercessor, Advocate, Strengthener, and Standby) who would remain with you forever (John 14:16) and live with you constantly and be in you (John 14:17) after My death and resurrection.

My Holy Spirit lives in you (1 Corinthians 3:16). My Spirit is special and wants you to speak to Him in tongues. He will intercede what is spoken to Me and I will take it to our Father. We are a three part being Father, Son, and Holy Spirit. We all work together for your benefit.

Father, I thank You for sending Jesus. Jesus, I thank You for the Holy Spirit. Holy Spirit, I thank You for the baptism of the Holy Spirit with the evidence of speaking in tongues. In Jesus' name Amen.

❖DAY 6❖
Read 1 Corinthians 14:1-5; Jude 1:20
John 14-16

Speaking in tongues charges your spirit like a battery charger charges a battery. It gives strength to your body and power within you. There are many benefits of praying in tongues. Don't let the devil talk you out of it or put fear in you. Ask Me to fill you and I will and you will feel the river bubble up in you. Certain syllables will come to mind and you just need to speak them out.

Practice praying in tongues daily as much as you can and out of your heart will flow rivers of living water (John 7:38). Don't be drunk with wine but ever be filled *and* stimulated with My Spirit (Ephesians 5:18). Being filled with My Spirit is a continual filling. It is not a one-time event.

Father, I declare I will not fear speaking in tongues. I ask You, Father to fill me to overflowing with evidence of praying in tongues. In Jesus' name Amen.

Read 1 Corinthians 14:1-5; Jude 1:20
John 14-16

1. What is the purpose of praying in tongues?

2. If speaking in tongues in a church service, what must you have?

3. When praying in tongues the Holy Spirit doesn't pray, instead He does what?

4. What will the Spirit reveal to you as you pray in tongues?

5. What did Jesus ask the Father to give you?

6. Speaking in tongues charges your spirit like what and what does it give you?

NOTES:

WEEK 38
❖RIVER OF LIVING WATER❖
෬෬෬෬෬෬෬෬෬෬෬෬෬෬෬෬෬

❖DAY 1❖
Read Ezekiel 47:1-12; John 7:37-39

I am going to compare the river in Ezekiel to My Spirit and your life as a believer from the beginning when you accepted Me as your Lord and Savior. Before you were born again it was like being on the shore of this river. You were lost, broken, and without hope. You made the decision to live for Me and stepped into this river. When you were first born again you were ankle deep in spiritual things.

It takes a while to grow in Me and My Word, but if you stay in My Word and in fellowship with other believers, you will grow. You received My Spirit when you were born again, but not baptized in My Spirit yet with evidence of speaking in tongues. That is a separate experience.

Father, I declare I will continue to grow in You and Your Word as I meditate on Your Word. In Jesus' name Amen.

❖DAY 2❖
Read Ezekiel 47:1-12; John 7:37-39

As you continue on this spiritual journey in the river, you are now knee deep in spiritual things. You are starting to read My Word more and are in a Bible study. There is so much you don't understand, but you desire to know more.

Keep in fellowship with other believers and stay in My Word. You need to find a time to be with Me. Talk to Me as a friend and you will receive blessings.

Father, I declare I am knee deep in my growing in You and desire to go deeper. In Jesus' name Amen.

❖DAY 3❖
Read Ezekiel 47:1-12; John 7:37-39

As you continue on you are now waist deep in spiritual things. You've learned so much but are hungry for so much more. You read in My Word that I am love and love you more than you can even imagine.

It's hard for you to realize how much I love you especially with everything that is going on in your life, the hurts and the sicknesses, and all the bad things that seem to be happening. I am for you not against you. My love dwells within you as well as My healing power. It was given to you on the cross the same as salvation. Never doubt My love for you.

Father, I thank You for Your love for me. I declare Your love dwells in me and You are for me and not against me. In Jesus' name Amen.

❖DAY 4❖
Read Ezekiel 47:1-12; John 7:37-39

As you continue on this journey, you feel spiritual things are way too deep for you but discovered the baptism of My Spirit with evidence of speaking in tongues. You jumped in the river because it was too deep to continue walking in and feel so alive and overjoyed with My presence.

The more you pray in My Spirit, the more powerful you feel and stirred up in your spirit. As you continue in My Word, revelation and understanding starts coming to you and you are becoming freer in Me.

Father, I declare I pray in the Spirit and receive revelation and understanding and edification in my spirit. Thank You Lord. In Jesus' name Amen.

❖DAY 5❖
Read Ezekiel 47:1-12; John 7:37-39

As you flow in this river, you start bearing fruit and receive healing. You feel nothing can keep you down. As you read My Word, you discover you have authority in My name against the devil and his schemes. You realize you don't have to put up with the bad that the devil tries to dish out and that he can only get to you if you allow him.

It's the same with sickness, it is from the devil. You discovered it is My will to heal. The devil comes to steal, kill, and destroy. I come to give you life abundantly (John 10:10).

Father, I declare I am bearing fruit for Your kingdom and I am healed. I have power and authority over the devil in Your name. In Jesus' name Amen.

❖DAY 6❖
Read Ezekiel 47:1-12; John 7:37-39

Praying in My Spirit is like a bubbling spring flowing out of you which illustrates the difference between your new birth and your experience of the overflowing fullness of the Spirit-filled life. You have become a channel of spiritual refreshment for others.

You notice the difference from when you were first born again and now that you are baptized in My Spirit with evidence of praying in tongues. Continue in your prayer language and continue in My Word and fellowship with other believers. You will be like a tree on the sides of this river that will not wither, turn brown or die and it continues to bear fruit. You will continue to bear fruit and will become a powerful intercessor.

Father, I am so excited to be filled with the Spirit and praying in tongues. I feel stirred up and bubbling over with Your love and power. Thank You for the baptism of the Holy Spirit and praying in tongues. In Jesus' name Amen.

Read Ezekiel 47:1-12; John 7:37-39

1. What is being compared to the river in Ezekiel 47?

2. What is going on as you are knee deep?

3. What do you realize as you are waist deep in this river?

4. What happened when you couldn't walk in the river anymore?

5. What do you start doing as you flow in this river?

6. What is praying in the Holy Spirit like? What will you be like as you continue on this spiritual journey?

NOTES:

WEEK 39
❖NOT GIVEN A SPIRIT OF FEAR❖

❖DAY 1❖
Read 2 Timothy 1:7; 1 John 4:18; Hebrews 13:6
Matthew 10:26-33; Romans 8:15; Psalm 27:1

I have not given you a spirit of fear but of power, love, and a sound mind. What is a spirit of fear? It is spirits that cause torment or have a dread about something. Fear will cause you to take flight and tremble uncontrollably. In Me, you do not have to fear.

I am love and perfect love casts out fear and torment. My love is in you. I hold you securely and the evil one cannot touch you (1 John 5:18).

Father, I declare You have not given me a spirit of fear but of power, love, and a sound mind. Thank You for holding me securely so that the evil one cannot touch me. In Jesus' name Amen.

❖DAY 2❖
Read 2 Timothy 1:7; 1 John 4:18; Hebrews 13:6
Matthew 10:26-33; Romans 8:15; Psalm 27:1

You can have confidence in Me because I am your helper and you do not have to fear what man can do to you. You sometimes fear what others will think and not obey My Word because of the intimidation of others. You will not speak up about things of faith because of what others may think or do.

Do not fear them. Have trust and confidence in Me. I will come running when you cry out for My help.

Father, I declare I have confidence in You to help me when I cry out for Your help. I will not fear what man can do to me. In Jesus' name Amen.

❖DAY 3❖
Read 2 Timothy 1:7; 1 John 4:18; Hebrews 13:6
Matthew 10:26-33; Romans 8:15; Psalm 27:1

Don't be afraid of those who threaten you. I will reveal truth and expose all that is in darkness. Don't fear man but fear Me which means to reverence Me.

You don't have to be afraid of Me or have a fear of Me. I am for you, not against you. I love you more than you can ever imagine. I am with you and will never leave you. Do not fear what man can do to you.

Father, I declare I will not be afraid of what man can do to me. I will fear and reverence You and walk in victory and peace. In Jesus' name Amen.

❖DAY 4❖
Read 2 Timothy 1:7; 1 John 4:18; Hebrews 13:6
Matthew 10:26-33; Romans 8:15; Psalm 27:1

You are more valuable to Me than the sparrows. I watch out for the sparrows and every kind of bird. If I take care of the sparrow, don't you think I would take care of you?

You are more valuable to Me than a whole flock of sparrows. Every hair on your head is numbered. So do not fear, I will take care of you.

Father, I declare I am more valuable to you than a whole flock of sparrows. Every hair on my head is numbered. Thank You, Lord, for taking care of me. In Jesus' name Amen.

❖DAY 5❖
Read 2 Timothy 1:7; 1 John 4:18; Hebrews 13:6
Matthew 10:26-33; Romans 8:15; Psalm 27:1

Let not your heart be troubled, trust in Me and I will take care of you. Cast all your care on Me for I care for you (I Peter 5:7).

If you have any fear come upon you, I have not given it to you. You are not being led by My Spirit if you are in fear. Submit to Me and resist the devil who puts this fear in you and he will flee from you (James 4:7).

Father, I declare I will not let my heart be troubled or afraid, I will trust in You. I will cast all my cares upon You. I will submit to You and resist the devil and he will flee from me. In Jesus' name Amen.

❖DAY 6❖
Read 2 Timothy 1:7; 1 John 4:18; Hebrews 13:6
Matthew 10:26-33; Romans 8:15; Psalm 27:1

I am your light and salvation you have no need to be afraid. I am your fortress and I will protect you from danger. Trust Me and do not fear. I will give you peace.

Stay in My Word and close to Me. You have nothing to fear even with all that is going on in this world. I am with you and will never leave you. I will protect you as long as you stay close to Me and resist any fear that comes your way.

Father, I declare I will not be afraid, because You are my light and my salvation. You are my fortress and will protect me from danger as long as I stay in Your Word and stay close to You. I will resist any fear that comes my way. In Jesus' name Amen.

Read 2 Timothy 1:7; 1 John 4:18; Hebrews 13:6
Matthew 10:26-33; Romans 8:15; Psalm 27:1

1. What is a spirit of fear and where does it come from?

2. Why can we have confidence in God?

3. What does fear of the Lord mean?

4. You are more valuable to God than what?

5. Why are you not to let your heart be troubled?

6. Why do you have no need to be afraid? How can we be protected from danger?

NOTES:

WEEK 40
❖HOLY SPIRIT POWER ❖
ぺぺぺぺぺぺぺぺぺぺぺぺぺぺぺ

❖DAY 1❖
Read Acts 1:8; Ephesians 1:19-20; Luke 9:1; 10:19
2 Corinthians 4:7; 1 Corinthians 2:5

I have not given you a spirit of fear but I have given you power, love, and a sound mind. My Holy Spirit empowers you to minister to others. Without this power, you will be ineffective. My power is available to every believer. Ask and you shall receive.

This power will help you to keep the spirit of fear from you. You must realize My power dwells within you because Holy Spirit dwells within you.

Father, I declare You have not given me a spirit of fear but a spirit of power. Holy Spirit empowers me to minister as He leads me. Your power and Holy Spirit dwells within me. In Jesus' name Amen.

❖DAY 2❖
Read Acts 1:8; Ephesians 1:19-20; Luke 9:1; 10:19
2 Corinthians 4:7; 1 Corinthians 2:5

My power is available to you through faith. As you experience My immense power, it will be an advertisement to others as it works through you.

This mighty power is what raised Me from the dead and exalted Me to the place of highest honor and supreme authority in the heavenly realm.

Father, I declare Your power is available to me through faith. As I experience this immense power, it will be an advertisement to others as it works through me. Thank You for this immense power. In Jesus name Amen.

165

❖DAY 3❖
Read Acts 1:8; Ephesians 1:19-20; Luke 9:1; 10:19
2 Corinthians 4:7; 1 Corinthians 2:5

This power that raised Me from the dead dwells in you permeating through your veins sending healing throughout your body. This power heals, delivers, and sets you free by My Holy Spirit.

Get this revelation of My power and you will walk in victory in every area of your life. It is available to you.

Father, I declare the power that raised Jesus from the dead dwells within me permeating through my veins sending healing throughout my body. It heals, delivers, and sets me free. As I get the revelation of this great power, I will walk in victory in every area of my life. In Jesus' name Amen.

❖DAY 4❖
Read Acts 1:8; Ephesians 1:19-20; Luke 9:1; 10:19
2 Corinthians 4:7; 1 Corinthians 2:5

I gave power and authority to the disciples as well as to you over every demon and the power to heal every disease. I gave you the authority over sickness, disease, and pain even in your own body. You have the authority to command it to leave.

Also, I have given the power and authority to minister to others with sickness and disease. My Church is destroyed from lack of knowledge of the authority and power you have been given (Hosea 4:6). Get this revelation and walk in victory.

Father, I declare I have the revelation that you have given me power and authority over every demon and power to heal every disease in myself and to minister to others. In Jesus' name Amen.

166

Read Acts 1:8; Ephesians 1:19-20; Luke 9:1; 10:19
2 Corinthians 4:7; 1 Corinthians 2:5

My disciples came back full of joy that demons obeyed them when they commanded them to leave in My name. While they ministered, I watched Satan topple until he fell suddenly from heaven like lightning to the ground. I see the same when you command them to leave in My name.

As you understand that I imparted to you all my authority to trample over Satan's kingdom, you will trample upon every demon before you and overcome every power Satan possesses. Nothing will be able to harm you as you walk in My authority (Luke 10:19 Passion Translation).

Father, I declare I understand You imparted to me all Your authority to trample over Satan's kingdom. I will trample upon every demon before me and overcome every power Satan possesses. Nothing will harm me as I walk in Your authority. In Jesus' name Amen.

❖DAY 6❖
Read Acts 1:8; Ephesians 1:19-20; Luke 9:1; 10:19
2 Corinthians 4:7; 1 Corinthians 2:5

You are like a clay jar that carries My glorious treasure within you. This power is to be seen as My power, not yours.

I intended for your faith to be established on trusting in My almighty power not on man's wisdom. Flow in My Holy Spirit power and victory will be yours always.

Father, I declare I am like a clay jar that carries Your glorious treasure within me. I will walk in Your power, not mine. My faith is established on trusting in Your almighty power. In Jesus' name Amen.

Read Acts 1:8; Ephesians 1:19-20; Luke 9:1; 10:19
2 Corinthians 4:7; 1 Corinthians 2:5

1. God has not given us a spirit of fear but of what?

2. As you experience God's power, what will it be to others?

3. Where does the power that raised Jesus from the dead dwell?

4. What has Jesus given us power over?

5. As you understand that Jesus imparted His power and authority to you, what will you be able to do?

6. You are like a clay jar carrying what?

NOTES:

WEEK 41
❖LOVE AND SOUND MIND❖
~~~~~~~~~~~~~~~~~~~~~~~~~

❖DAY 1❖
Read Ephesians 3:14-21; Isaiah 26:3; Luke 12:22-34
Philippians 4:8; 1 Corinthians 2:16

I have not given you a spirit of fear but of power, love, and a sound mind. My love for you is more than you will ever realize. I want you to experience My unconditional love in every dimension of it. My love is poured into you so you are filled to overflowing with My fullness. You must be rooted and grounded in My love. It must go deep as tree roots go deep for it to grow. My love is the foundation of everything.

I am love and you can experience an intimate knowledge of Me. Trust in My love for you. My perfect love will drive fear far from you. So walk in My love, demonstrate My love to others and be free (1 John 4).

Father, I want to experience every dimension of Your love. Your love is poured into me and I am filled to overflowing with the fullness of You. I am rooted and grounded in Your love. I desire an intimate knowledge of You and I trust Your love for me. I will not fear because Your perfect love drives out fear. In Jesus' name Amen.

❖DAY 2❖
Read Ephesians 3:14-21; Isaiah 26:3; Luke 12:22-34
Philippians 4:8; 1 Corinthians 2:16

I have given you a sound mind. A sound mind is a mind that has good judgment, disciplined thought patterns, and the ability to understand and make right decisions and self-control. You have a sound mind and perfect peace when your thoughts are fixed on Me and you trust Me in all that you do.

Father, I declare I have a sound mind that has safe thinking, good judgment, disciplined thought patterns and the ability to understand and make right decisions. I trust You Lord in all things. In Jesus' name Amen.

❖DAY 3❖
Read Ephesians 3:14-21; Isaiah 26:3; Luke 12:22-34
Philippians 4:8; 1 Corinthians 2:16

Do not worry about anything or have an anxious mind. An anxious mind is one that is worried and thinking about the worst. Think on positive things.

Consider the birds that do not reap or store. I feed them and take care of them. You are much more valuable to Me than the birds. Seek My kingdom and all the things you need and My promises will be added to you.

Father, I declare I will not worry or have an anxious mind. I will think on positive things and seek Your kingdom and all things and Your promises will be added to me. In Jesus' name Amen.

❖DAY 4❖
Read Ephesians 3:14-21; Isaiah 26:3; Luke 12:22-34
Philippians 4:8; 1 Corinthians 2:16

Character and conduct begin in your mind. Your actions are affected by what you think and dwell on. You are to concentrate on things that will result in right living and in My peace.

Think on whatever is true. My Word is truth, not the report you received from the doctor or the red in your bank account. Think about what My Word says about these things. Speak those things that you desire, not the things in the natural that you have.

Think on things that are honorable and decent. If you are watching the news all the time, it will be hard to think about things that are decent and honorable. Think on My Word which is honorable and decent.

Father, I declare I will concentrate on things that will result in right living and in peace. I will think on things that are true and honorable and right. I will think on Your Word. In Jesus' name Amen.

Read Ephesians 3:14-21; Isaiah 26:3; Luke 12:22-34
Philippians 4:8; 1 Corinthians 2:16

Think on things that are just and right. The things of this world are not just and right. I am just and right. Set your thoughts on Me.

Think on things that are pure which are holy, clean, modest, undefiled, and morally faultless, and without blemish. Since I was able to overcome temptation, I remain pure and spotless. I am your pure and spotless lamb and I take away all your sins on the cross.

Father, I declare I will think on things that are just and right. I will think on You Lord and not on the things in the world. I will think on things that are pure and holy. Jesus is pure and holy, my pure and spotless lamb that takes away all my sins. In Jesus' name Amen.

Read Ephesians 3:14-21; Isaiah 26:3; Luke 12:22-34
Philippians 4:8; 1 Corinthians 2:16

Think on things that are lovely and beautiful. There are some things in this world that are lovely. The birds, trees, scenery, and nature are lovely things to think about. I have created beautiful things for you on this earth. Think on these things, but mostly on heavenly things.

Think on things of good report which is what My Word says about your situations in life. A bad report would be what the doctor told you or the red ink in your bank account. Whose report will you believe? Believe and think on My report, on My Word.

Think of things that are excellent and worthy of praise. Think on My deeds and give praise. Meditate on these things and you will have My mind and understanding of our Father.

Father, I declare I will think on things that are lovely and beautiful. I will think of things of good report and things that are excellent and worthy of praise. As I meditate on these things, I have the mind of Christ and His understanding. In Jesus' name Amen.

Read Ephesians 3:14-21; Isaiah 26:3; Luke 12:22-34
Philippians 4:8; 1 Corinthians 2:16

1. What kind of love drives out fear?

2. What is a sound mind?

3. What is an anxious mind?

4. What begins in your mind? What are things that are true, honorable and decent?

5. What are things that are just, right and pure?

6. What are things that are lovely, beautiful, and of good report? What is excellent and praise worthy? How do you think on these things?

NOTES:

WEEK 42
❖ROCK AND STRENGTH❖
❧❧❧❧❧❧❧❧❧❧❧❧❧❧❧❧

❖DAY 1❖
Read Psalm 18:2; Matthew 7: 24-27
Psalm 46:1; Philippians 4:13; Nehemiah 8:10

I am your rock and your strength. A rock is a solid substance that gives support and foundation. You can find refuge in Me. I will protect you if you build upon the foundation that I provide as your rock.

I am your shield that will protect you from the fiery darts of the wicked one. I am here for you no matter what you go through. I will go through it with you and you will have the victory.

Father, I declare You are my rock and my strength. I find refuge and protection in You as I build upon the solid foundation that You provide. You are a shield that protects me from the fiery darts of the wicked one. Thank You for never leaving me or forsaking me. In Jesus' name Amen.

❖DAY 2❖
Read Psalm 18:2; Matthew 7:24-27
Psalm 46:1; Philippians 4:13; Nehemiah 8:10

You are a wise person if you listen to My Words and follow them. You are like a house that is built on a rock. When the winds beat against this house and the rains come, it is able to stand because it is built on the rock.

If you don't listen to My Words and follow them you will be foolish like the house built on sand. When the winds beat against this house and the rains come, it will collapse with a mighty crash. If this is the way your life seems, check to see if you are obeying My Words and following after Me.

Father, I declare I will be like a wise person and listen to Your Words and follow after them so that I can be like the house built on the rock when the storms come my way. I will not be foolish like the house built on the sand. In Jesus' name Amen.

173

❖DAY 3❖
Read Psalm 18:2; Matthew 7:24-27
Psalm 46:1; Philippians 4:13; Nehemiah 8:10

I am your refuge and strength. A very present help when you are in trouble. Do not fear when you see troubles surround you. I dwell within you and I am present when the storms come. I will protect you and keep you safe in the midst of the storm.

I never promised that storms wouldn't come your way but I have promised to protect you and be your refuge as long as you stay within My shelter.

Father, I declare you are my refuge and strength. You are a very present help when I am in trouble. I will not fear when troubles surround me. You will protect me and keep me safe. I will stay in Your shelter. In Jesus' name Amen.

❖DAY 4❖
Read Psalm 18:2; Matthew 7:24-27
Psalm 46:1; Philippians 4:13; Nehemiah 8:10

I am your strength. I give you power and security. You can do all things through Me because I give you strength. It is only possible by you being connected to Me and Me to you as the branch and the vine are connected (John 15:5).

How do you get this connection? You must meditate in My Word daily and seek My face.

Father, I declare You give me strength, power, and security. I can do all things through Jesus because He gives me strength. I meditate on Your Word and seek Your face. In Jesus' name Amen.

❖DAY 5❖
Read Psalm 18:2; Matthew 7:24-27
Psalm 46:1; Philippians 4:13; Nehemiah 8:10

My joy is your strength. Happiness and joy are two different things. Happiness comes from outward things in your life; joy comes from your heart, from My Holy Spirit living in you.

Understanding and obeying Scripture brings joy to your lives and teaches you to acknowledge My hand in your success. Just knowing My Word and My presence will give you joy and through this joy, you will be strengthened.

Father, I declare the joy of the Lord is my strength. I will obey Your Word and receive Your joy and strength. In Jesus' name Amen.

❖DAY 6❖
Read Psalm 18:2; Matthew 7:24-27
Psalm 46:1; Philippians 4:13; Nehemiah 8:10

My grace is sufficient for you, for My strength is made perfect in weakness (2 Corinthians 12:9). This word grace in this verse is the root word meaning joy or to rejoice. Grace, My unmerited favor, is a manifestation of My power exceeding what you could achieve or hope for by your own labors. It is effective at salvation but also a resource that makes possible to do things when you are under fire from the adversary.

My grace becomes your enablement or empowerment to achieve My plan, endure hardship, or have access to Me. My grace helps your abilities to conquer every weakness as you yield to Me and have complete trust and reliance upon Me. You can take pleasure in your weaknesses because I will give you strength to endure.

Father, I declare Your grace is sufficient for me for Your strength is made perfect in my weakness. Thank You for empowering me to overcome. In Jesus' name Amen.

175

❖DAY 7-SUMMARY QUESTIONS❖
Read Psalm 18:2; Matthew 7:24-27
Psalm 46:1; Philippians 4:13; Nehemiah 8:10

1. God will protect us if we build our life upon what?

2. You are a wise person if you do what?

3. God is your what?

4. What must you do to be connected to Jesus?

5. What is your strength? What is the difference between joy and happiness?

6. What is grace and what does it provide?

NOTES:

WEEK 43
❖GOD'S MERCY❖
ೞೞೞೞೞೞೞೞೞೞ

❖DAY 1❖
Read Exodus 34:6; Psalm 145:8; Psalm 136:1
Ephesians 2:4; Matthew 14:14; 9:36-38

I am a God of compassion and mercy. I am slow to anger and filled with unfailing love and faithfulness. I am moved by compassion toward you. Because of My compassion, My heart yearns to meet your needs.

When you act on My Word it puts you in a position of receiving My mercy. Mercy is the outward expression of the inward compassion.

Father, I declare You are a God of compassion and mercy. I will act on Your Word so I will be in a position to receive Your mercy. Thank You. In Jesus' name Amen.

❖DAY 2❖
Read Exodus 34:6; Psalm 145:8; Psalm 136:1
Ephesians 2:4; Matthew 14:14; 9:36-38

I want you to know that I am not mad at you or angry with you when you fail. I am slow to anger and have great mercy toward you. Trust My love and mercy and you will have victory in your life.

Stop beating yourself up when you fail; just get into My Word and into My presence and everything will be alright.

Father, I declare You are not mad at me or angry at me when I fail. You have love and great mercy toward me when I fail. I will get into Your Word and Your presence and everything will be alright. In Jesus' name Amen.

❖DAY 3❖
Read Exodus 34:6; Psalm 145:8; Psalm 136:1
Ephesians 2:4; Matthew 14:14; 9:36-38

Give thanks to our Father God for He is good. Our Father God loves you so much He sent Me to die for your sins so that you will live forever and be forgiven. He is a good, good Father and His mercy endures forever.

Forever is eternal. His mercy never runs out. He is faithful to keep His covenant and to offer His mercy (Deuteronomy 7:9). He is always ready to forgive because of My shed blood on the cross.

Father, I declare I will give thanks to You because You are good and Your mercy endures forever and ever. You are a good, good Father and always ready to forgive me for all of my sins. Thank You. In Jesus' name Amen.

❖DAY 4❖
Read Exodus 34:6; Psalm 145:8; Psalm 136:1
Ephesians 2:4; Matthew 14:14; 9:36-38

Father God is so rich in mercy and loves you so very, very much. He gave you life when He raised Me from the dead and you are seated with Me in heavenly places.

Since My Spirit dwells in you, you are to walk in love and compassion toward others. My love, compassion, and mercy dwell within you to be released to others. Be moved with compassion and have mercy on those in need, reaching out to them.

Father, I declare You are so rich in mercy and love me very much. You gave me life when You raised Jesus from the dead. I will be moved with compassion for others, have mercy on them and reach out to them because Your love, compassion, and mercy dwells in me. In Jesus' name Amen.

❖DAY 5❖
Read Exodus 34:6; Psalm 145:8; Psalm 136:1
Ephesians 2:4; Matthew 14:14; 9:36-38

An example of My compassion as I walked on this earth was when I got out of the boat the crowd was waiting for Me and I had compassion on them and healed all their sick.

I loved the people so much and saw their need; I just had to minister to them. I could not send them away even though I had just heard about John the Baptist being beheaded. Sometimes you need to see the other person and their need rather than your own.

Father, I declare I will walk in compassion and have mercy on others no matter what is going on in my life. I will love them and minister to them. In Jesus' name Amen.

❖DAY 6❖
Read Exodus 34:6; Psalm 145:8; Psalm 136:1
Ephesians 2:4; Matthew 14:14; 9:36-38

Another example is as I went from town to town; I saw the multitude of people and healed all that were sick. I had compassion on them because they were confused and helpless, like sheep without a shepherd.

There are a lot of people in the world today just like those people and they need someone to reach out to them with compassion. The harvest is great but the workers are few. Pray for more laborers to be sent out to the harvest.

People need you to have compassion and mercy on them. They are lost and you are to help them find their way. You have the answer for the world today. I am the way. You are My representative in this world. Tell them about Me and My love.

Father, I declare I will have love and compassion on those in need. I will tell others of Your love and that You are the answer for them. I will pray for more laborers to be sent out to the harvest. In Jesus' name Amen.

179

1. What puts you in the position of receiving God's mercy?

2. Is God mad or angry at you?

3. Why is God always ready to forgive you?

4. Where does God's love, compassion, and mercy dwell?

5. What did Jesus do for the crowd when He got out of the boat?

6. What are you to pray for and what are you to do as Jesus' representative on the earth?

NOTES:

WEEK 44
❖KNOW GOD'S VOICE❖
꒤꒤꒤꒤꒤꒤꒤꒤꒤꒤꒤꒤

❖DAY 1❖
Read Genesis 1; John 1:1-5
John 10: 11-29

In Genesis 1:1 My Spirit was hovering over the water. Father God was speaking to Holy Spirit and to the formless and empty places. When He spoke, it was. Day 1 through 6, He spoke and it was.

On the 6ᵗʰ day, He said, "Let us make man in our image." Our Father God, Myself, and Holy Spirit are all three working together so Father God is referring to Me, My Holy Spirit, and Himself when He speaks of creating man in "our image", meaning you are a spirit.

Father, I declare when You spoke, it was. You created man in Your image meaning I am a spirit. In Jesus' name Amen.

❖DAY 2❖
Read Genesis 1; John 1:1-5
John 10: 11-29

I was the Word in the beginning with Father God. I was the divine agent who was responsible for the entire creation. During this whole creation, Father God was speaking to Me and Holy Spirit and everything came into being. Father God spoke; I and Holy Spirit listened and it came into being. We all worked together.

In Genesis 2:17, Father God speaks to the man. He commands him to freely eat from any tree in the garden except for the tree of the knowledge of good and evil. They would surely die if they did.

Father, I declare Jesus was the Word in the beginning with You. He was the divine agent who was responsible for the entire creation. You, Jesus and the Holy Spirit worked together in creation. He spoke to Adam and gave him instructions just as You do today with me. In Jesus' name Amen.

❖DAY 3❖
Read Genesis 1; John 1:1-5
John 10: 11-29

We brought all the animals before Adam and had him name them. We were communicating with Adam and we were working together. We asked Adam, "What do you want to call this funny looking creature?" He named them all.

In Genesis 3, Adam and Eve had a conversation with Satan which is something you don't want to do, other than commanding him to leave you alone. I give you that authority in My name. He deceived them into eating of the tree of the knowledge of good and evil. They died spiritually at that time and were banished from the garden.

Because of the curse brought on by Adam and Eve's disobedience, communion with Us was not done without our initiative. Man's covering, which was Father God's glory, was gone from them and they lost that intimate communion with Us.

Father, I declare You communed with Adam in the garden and helped him name the animals. I declare I will not have a conversation with Satan as Adam and Eve did. I will not be deceived by Satan. I will use my authority in Jesus' name against him. In Jesus' name Amen.

❖DAY 4❖
Read Genesis 1; John 1:1-5
John 10: 11-29

In the Old Testament, My Spirit did not dwell in the people as in believers today. They heard our voice audibly. We also spoke in dreams and visions.

Today, as a born-again believer in Me, My Spirit dwells within you and speaks to you in your spirit. You must learn how to hear Me in your spirit. It will be a prompting, an impression, a thought, an inward witness, a leading or unction from your spirit. Also, I speak through My written Word and dreams and visions.

Father, I declare I hear Your voice in my spirit by a prompting, an impression, a thought, an inward witness, a leading, unction from my spirit or from Your written Word. In Jesus' name Amen.

❖DAY 5❖
Read Genesis 1; John 1:1-5
John 10:11-29

I am Your good shepherd. You are My sheep. Sheep always follow the shepherd and know the shepherd's voice. They will not follow a stranger's voice. You know My voice and are to follow Me. Hear Me and obey. There is no other way to victory.

I have revealed Myself in your spirit. You learn to hear Me in your spirit and know Me by My Word. You need to have a teachable, hearing heart.

Father, I declare You are the good shepherd, I am Your sheep. I will hear and know Your voice and follow after You only. I will learn to hear You in my spirit and know Your Word. In Jesus' name Amen.

❖DAY 6❖
Read Genesis 1; John 1:1-5
John 10:11-29

The only way My Word will ever do you any good is for you to live by what you hear. You have to be willing to make adjustments so that you act in agreement with what I say.

When you hear My voice, you will feel rested and peaceful. You will feel good about yourself. You will feel special, empowered, and courageous. You will feel loved. My voice will affect you like a cool mountain stream. It refreshes and invigorates you and honors your free will.

Satan's voice will make you feel defeated, isolated, hopeless, cynical about life and full of despair. You may feel you have to take matters into your own hands. Satan has a way of spoiling your attitude so you will turn your concentration away from Me and lose your sense of closeness to Me. He will make you feel like you lost your will, a feeling that you can't stop what you are doing. Satan tempts you to make quick, rash decisions. Satan comes to steal, kill, and destroy. I come to give you an abundant joyful life.

Father, I will live by what You tell me. I will make adjustments to be in agreement with Your Word. In Jesus' name Amen.

❖DAY 7-SUMMARY QUESTIONS❖
Read Genesis 1; John 1:1-5
John 10:11-29

1. Who is God referring to when He says He is to make man in "our image"?

2. What command did God speak to Adam to not do?

3. What happened after Adam and Eve sinned?

4. Where do you need to hear God's voice?

5. Where does God reveal Himself to you?

6. How will you feel when you hear the voice of God? How will you feel when you hear Satan's voice?

NOTES:

WEEK 45
❖SIGNS FOLLOWING YOU❖

❖DAY 1❖
Read Mark 16:15-20; John 14:12-24

I told the disciples and I tell you to go preach the Word to everyone. I know you are saying, "I am not a preacher". You may not be a preacher of the five-fold ministry, but you are to be My representative on the earth and tell everyone what happened to you when you accepted Me as your Lord and Savior. You are My representative on the earth, no matter where you are.

As you go out and minister to others as My witnesses, you will have signs and wonders following you.

Father, I declare I am Your representative on this earth and I am to go out and tell others about You and what happened to me when I accepted You as my Lord and Savior. As I do, signs and wonders will follow me. In Jesus' name Amen.

❖DAY 2❖
Read Mark 16:15-20; John 14:12-24

When you accepted Me as your Lord and Savior, I have given you the power and authority in My name to do the things that I did while on the earth, even greater things because I have gone to the Father and sent you My Holy Spirit to live in you and help you.

The signs and wonders that will follow you are: in My name you will be able to cast out demons, speak with new tongues, take up serpents, drink anything deadly, and it will not harm you. You will lay hands on the sick and they will recover.

Father, I declare You have given me power and authority in Your name to do the things You did while on the earth and even greater things than these. Signs and wonders will follow me as I represent You. In Jesus' name Amen.

185

❖DAY 3❖
Read Mark 16:15-20; John 14:12-24

The first sign and wonder is the ability to cast out demons. Resist the devil and he will flee from you. The devil was defeated when I died on the cross and rose from the grave. The only power he has is what you give to him.

You can cast demons out of others who want to be free. In My name the demons must listen to you and flee. Do not fear. In Me you are more powerful than they are. Examples of demons being cast out are in Matthew 17:18, Luke 4:41, Mark 1:34, Luke 13:32, Luke 10:17-20.

Father, I declare I will resist the devil and he has to flee from me. You give me the authority in Your name to cast out demons from others who want to be free. In Jesus' name Amen.

❖DAY 4❖
Read Mark 16:15-20; John 14:12-24

Praying in tongues or in My Spirit is a sign and wonder. It is a spiritual, supernatural language that speaks from your spirit to My Spirit. I talked about this in weeks 36 and 37.

It gives you the power and ability to overcome the devil because he doesn't know what you are praying to Me. It is also a gift of My Spirit which I will talk about later. It edifies you (Jude 1:20).

Father, I declare praying in the Spirit is a sign and wonder. It is a spiritual, supernatural language You have given me speaking to Your Spirit from my spirit. It gives me power and the ability to overcome the devil because he doesn't know what I am praying. It is a gift of Your Spirit and it edifies me. In Jesus' name Amen.

❖DAY 5❖
Read Mark 16:15-20; John 14:12-24

You can pick up serpents and drink anything deadly and it will not hurt you. This is not picking up snakes to prove My authority in your life but if you accidently pick up a deadly snake it will not hurt you.

An example is in Acts 28:3-6 when Paul on the island of Malta gathered sticks and laid them on the fire. A viper came out because of the heat and fastened onto Paul's arm. He shook it off and it did not harm him.

It is the same for drinking anything deadly. Missionaries can depend on these signs and wonders wherever they are ministering. It is a good idea to bless your food to be protected.

Father, I declare if I pick up serpents or drink anything deadly it will not hurt me. I will pray over my food and will be protected from harm. In Jesus' name Amen.

❖DAY 6❖
Read Mark 16:15-20; John 14:12-24

The last sign and wonder that will follow you is that you will lay your hands on the sick and they will recover. While I walked the earth, most of My ministering was healing the sick and casting out demons.

In My name, you have the authority over sickness and disease in your life and in others. You are to heal the sick not just pray for them but with the power I have given you, heal them.

Speak as I have spoken to sickness. Speak as the disciples spoke to sickness as in Acts 3:1-9 where Peter and John told the lame man to rise up and walk. They didn't pray for him, they just told him in My name to rise up and walk. He rose up, stood and walked, leaping and praising Me. You are to do the same in My name.

Father, I declare I have power and authority in Your name to lay hands on the sick and they will recover. I will heal the sick by speaking in Your name and they will be healed. In Jesus' name Amen.

❖DAY 7-SUMMARY QUESTIONS❖
Read Mark 16:15-20; John 14:12-24

1. What will you have following you as you represent Jesus to others?

2. What are the signs and wonders that will follow you?

3. When was the devil defeated and what power does he have?

4. What does praying in the Spirit give you?

5. What happened to Paul on the island of Malta with the viper?

6. What do you have in the name of Jesus?

NOTES:

WEEK 46
❖GIFTS OF THE GODHEAD❖

❖DAY 1❖
Read Romans 12:2-8; Ephesians 4:11
1 Corinthians 12:8-10, 28

There are gifts of our Father God, gifts of Mine (Jesus), and gifts of My Holy Spirit. The Father's gifts are ministry, teaching, exhortation, giving, leadership, and mercy. These gifts are for basic life purpose and motivation.

My gifts are apostles, prophets, evangelist, pastor/teacher, and missionaries. These gifts are to facilitate and equip the body of the church.

My Holy Spirit gifts are word of wisdom, word of knowledge, faith, gifts of healing, working of miracles, prophesy, discerning of spirits, different kinds of tongues, and interpretation of tongues. These gifts are to profit the body of the church. I am going to talk this week and next week about My Holy Spirit gifts and how they help you and the body.

Father, thank You for all the gifts of the Godhead that are given to me to help me in expanding Your kingdom. In Jesus' name Amen.

❖DAY 2❖
Read Romans 12:2-8; Ephesians 4:11
1 Corinthians 12:8-10, 28

The first gift of My Spirit is the word of wisdom. This wisdom is not natural wisdom; when I see fit to reveal My own mind and purpose and plan to man in a supernatural way, I do it by this supernatural manifestation of the word of wisdom. It is not given to everyone but as My Spirit wills.

Thank You, Father, for the gift of the word of wisdom. It is given to man when You want to reveal Your own mind, purpose, and plan You do it by the manifestation of word of wisdom. In Jesus' name Amen.

❖DAY 3❖
Read Romans 12:2-8; Ephesians 4:11
1 Corinthians 12:8-10, 28

The next gift is the gift of word of knowledge. This gift is supernatural insight or understanding of circumstances or a body of facts by revelation pertaining to a person or event, given for a specific purpose, usually having to do with an immediate need.

Sometimes spiritual gifts work together. These two gifts, the word of wisdom and the word of knowledge operated throughout the Old Testament and the New Testament (1 Samuel 9; 1 Samuel 10:22; 1 Kings 18; 37, 38; 19:2. 14; 2 Kings 5: 21-26; John 4:7-26; Acts 5:1-4; 9:10-16; 8:26-29). There are many more examples of the word of wisdom and word of knowledge in operation.

Father, I declare the word of knowledge and the word of wisdom is available to me as you see fit when I need it ministering to others or even in my personal prayer time. Thank You Lord. In Jesus' name Amen.

❖DAY 4❖
Read Romans 12:2-8; Ephesians 4:11
1 Corinthians 12:8-10, 28

The next gift of the Spirit is the gift of faith or special faith. This is a supernatural ability to believe without doubt. You just know that you know that you have what you prayed for.

This faith is different than general faith or saving faith. It is also different than the faith mentioned in the fruit of the Spirit. Fruit of the Spirit faith is for character building and the gifts of the Spirit are for power.

Father, I declare I can operate in special faith as You give it to me when You see fit and when needed. In Jesus' name Amen.

190

❖DAY 5❖
Read Romans 12:2-8; Ephesians 4:11
1 Corinthians 12:8-10, 28

The next gift is the gift of healings which are manifested for the supernatural healing of sickness and disease without any natural source or means.

All these gifts are supernatural and given as I see fit. You may be praying for someone who needs healing and with the gift of healings, you lay your hands on the person and they will be instantly healed. I work through people who have faith and you will know when this gift is manifesting.

Father, I declare that the gift of healings is available to me as You see fit to supernaturally heal someone in need. In Jesus' name Amen.

❖DAY 6❖
Read Romans 12:2-8; Ephesians 4:11
1 Corinthians 12:8-10, 28

The next gift is the gift of working of miracles. This is supernatural power to intervene and counteract earthly and evil forces.

It is a power giving the ability to go beyond the natural. It operates closely with the gifts of faith and healings to bring authority over sin, Satan, sickness, and the binding forces of this age.

Father, I declare that working of miracles is supernatural power to intervene and counteract earthly and evil forces. It goes beyond the natural. It is given to me as You see fit. In Jesus' name Amen.

❖DAY 7-SUMMARY QUESTIONS❖
Read Romans 12:2-8; Ephesians 4:11
1 Corinthians 12:8-10, 28

1. What are the gifts of the Godhead?

2. What is the gift of the word of wisdom?

3. What is the gift of the word of knowledge?

4. What is the gift of faith? Is it the same as general or saving faith?

5. What is the gift of healings?

6. What is the gift of working of miracles?

NOTES:

WEEK 47
❖GIFTS OF THE HOLY SPIRIT❖
❧❧❧❧❧❧❧❧❧❧❧❧❧❧❧❧

❖DAY 1❖
Read 1 Corinthians 12:8-10, 28
1 Corinthians 14; 1 Corinthians 13:1-8

There are nine gifts of My Spirit and I talked about five of them last week so I will finish talking about My Holy Spirit gifts this week.

The sixth gift of My Spirit is prophecy. My Word says to pursue love and desire spiritual gifts, especially that you may prophesy. Everyone can prophesy but not everyone is a prophet. Prophecy is for edification, exhortation, and comfort of the congregation—corporately and individually.

Father, I declare I will pursue love and desire spiritual gifts especially that I may prophecy. In Jesus' name Amen.

❖DAY 2❖
Read 1 Corinthians 12:8-10, 28
1 Corinthians 14; 1 Corinthians 13:1-8

The next gift of My Spirit is discerning of spirits. This is the supernatural power to detect the realm of the spirits and their activity. This is not just discerning evil spirits but also good spirits such as John in Revelations.

Also, the discerning of spirits can be manifested to reveal the human spirit; that is, the good or evil tendencies of the human spirit. Discerning of spirits deals with three kind of classes of spirits: divine, satanic, and human.

Father, I declare I have available to me the gift of discerning of spirits, which gives me the ability to detect the realm of the spirit as the Holy Spirit wills. In Jesus' name Amen.

❖DAY 3❖
Read 1 Corinthians 12:8-10, 28
1 Corinthians 14; 1 Corinthians 13:1-8

The next gift is different kinds of tongues which is utterance in languages not known to the speaker. The church is edified when someone speaks with other tongues in the public assembly and there is an interpretation. Prophesy is equivalent to tongues and interpretation but is not greater.

Speaking with tongues and interpretation of tongues is for the unbeliever. It will convince them of the reality of the presence of God and often causes them to turn to Me and be saved (1 Corinthians 14:22). As with every gift, the gift of tongues operates only as the Spirit wills.

Father, I declare I am available to You to speak in tongues as You give me the utterance in a service to edify the church. In Jesus' name Amen.

❖DAY 4❖
Read 1 Corinthians 12:8-10, 28
1 Corinthians 14; 1 Corinthians 13:1-8

The last gift of the Spirit is the interpretation of tongues. The purpose of this gift is to give the gift of tongues understanding to the hearers so that the whole church may know what has been uttered in tongues and be edified.

The gift of interpretation is not a translation. It is showing forth supernaturally by the spirit of God the meaning of what was said in tongues. Tongues and interpretation must be done in order so there is no confusion but edification, inspiration, and blessing.

Father, I declare that I am available to You if interpretation is ever needed in church when tongues has been spoken. Thank You for the gifts of the Holy Spirit. In Jesus' name Amen.

❖DAY 5❖
Read 1 Corinthians 12:8-10, 28
1 Corinthians 14; 1 Corinthians 13:1-8

As mentioned before, all these gifts of My Spirit are given as My Spirit wills. You can't just say I am going to have a word of wisdom or word of knowledge for so and so. You can't just say I have the gift of faith regarding something or the gift of healings.

One and the same Spirit works all these gifts and distributing to each one as He wills. It is up to My Spirit who receives what and when. If you are baptized in My Spirit, you have access to all these gifts, but they are manifested as My Spirit wills.

Father, I declare that one and the same Spirit works all these gifts and distributes to each one as He wills. I declare I pursue love and desire the spiritual gifts. In Jesus' name Amen.

❖DAY 6❖
Read 1 Corinthians 12:8-10, 28
1 Corinthians 14; 1 Corinthians 13:1-8

My Word says in 1 Corinthians 13 that if you could speak in all the languages of men and angels but didn't love others, you would only be a noisy gong. If you had the gift of prophecy and you understood all of My secret plans and possessed all knowledge, and if you had such faith that you could move mountains but didn't love others, you would be nothing.

You can gain nothing without loving others. These gifts operate best when walking in My love.

Father, I declare I will walk in love and be motivated by Your love so that these gifts that are available to me will manifest in my life and benefit me and others. In Jesus' name Amen.

❖DAY 7-SUMMARY QUESTIONS❖
Read 1 Corinthians 12:8-10, 28
1 Corinthians 14; 1 Corinthians 13:1-8

1. What is prophecy?

2. What is discerning of spirits? What three classes of spirits does it deal with?

3. What are different kinds of tongues?

4. What is the purpose of interpretation of tongues? Is it a literal translation?

5. When are the gifts of the Spirit given?

6. These gifts operate best when you are walking in what?

NOTES:

WEEK 48
❖GOD IS WITH YOU ALWAYS❖

❖DAY 1❖

Read Hebrews 13:5-6; Deuteronomy 31:6-8, 23
Joshua 1:5-9; Psalm 27:1; 118:6-9

You can trust Me in every area of your life. You can be content and satisfied with what you have because I will never leave you nor forsake you.

You have nothing to fear because I am your helper in everything. You just need to cry out to Me and I will answer. You don't have to be afraid of anything or anyone. I am with you wherever you go.

Father, I declare I will trust You in every area of my life. I will be satisfied with what I have because You will never leave me nor forsake me. I will not fear anything or anyone because You are with me wherever I go. In Jesus' name Amen.

❖DAY 2❖

Read Hebrews 13:5-6; Deuteronomy 31:6-8, 23
Joshua 1:5-9; Psalm 27:1; 118:6-9

Sometimes you feel like I have abandoned you because of what may be going on in your life. Don't go by feelings. Trust Me and My Word. My Word says I will never leave you nor forsake you.

It's a matter of trust and faith. The Israelites saw My cloud by day and fire by night but still didn't have faith and trust in Me. They were still disobedient even though they could see the miraculous things I did for them.

Father, I declare I will not go by feelings but have faith and trust in You and Your Word that says You will never leave me nor forsake me. In Jesus' name Amen.

❖DAY 3❖
Read Hebrews 13:5-6; Deuteronomy 31:6-8, 23
Joshua 1:5-9; Psalm 27:1; 118:6-9

You can trust Me to never leave you because you are My temple and I dwell within you. In the Old Covenant, My Spirit did not dwell in believers. I came upon them but I did not dwell within them. You have a much better Covenant today.

You take Me wherever you go. Sometimes there are places you shouldn't go, that I am not comfortable in, but I am still with you because I dwell in you (1 Corinthians 6:19). In those times, My Spirit may convict you and lead you away from those places because it grieves My Spirit. I am still with you and will not leave you nor forsake you.

Father, I declare I will trust You because You dwell within me and will let me know if there is somewhere I shouldn't be, but You will never leave me nor forsake me even if I am somewhere I shouldn't be. In Jesus' name Amen.

❖DAY 4❖
Read Hebrews 13:5-6; Deuteronomy 31:6-8, 23
Joshua 1:5-9; Psalm 27:1; 118:6-9

In those times that you are where you should not be and are not obedient to the leading of My Spirit to leave that place, I cannot stop what may transpire. You must trust Me and have faith and always be obedient to the leading of My Spirit.

If My Spirit leads you to go a different route to get to work or wherever you are going and you do not obey that leading, I cannot stop the accident that may happen. That's the reason for the leading to go in another direction. Listen to My voice and you will have the victory in your life.

Father, I declare I will listen to the leading of Your Spirit and be obedient to Your leading and follow after You. In Jesus' name Amen.

❖DAY 5❖
Read Hebrews 13:5-6; Deuteronomy 31:6-8, 23
Joshua 1:5-9; Psalm 27:1; 118:6-9

In those times when you get into an accident or something bad happens, that is when you feel I have abandoned you. You wonder where I am at and why I allowed these things to happen.

I only allow you to choose rather to listen to Me or go your own way. Your own way may bring things into your life that you don't want. I am still with you through it all and will bring My will out of the bad, but if you obey the leading of My Spirit, good things can happen rather than bad.

Father, forgive me for the times I have not listened to Your voice and went my own way. I declare You are always with me no matter what transpires in my life. In Jesus' name Amen.

❖DAY 6❖
Read Hebrews 13:5-6; Deuteronomy 31:6-8, 23
Joshua 1:5-9; Psalm 27:1; 118:6-9

It is better to trust in Me than in other people. People can give you advice and counsel but please confide in Me before you make any decisions. I am your light and source of your salvation. You do not have to fear anything. I am with you and for you.

Listen to My voice. I am always speaking to you and desire you to speak to Me. I will help you to do what I lead you to do. I will never lead you to do anything without My support. Trust Me in all that you do. Acknowledge Me in all your ways and I will direct your paths. I love you and want the best for you.

Father, I declare I will trust You rather than other people. I will confide in You for direction. You are my light and the source of my salvation. I will not fear. I will acknowledge You in all my ways and You will direct my paths. Thank You Lord. I love You. In Jesus' name Amen.

Read Hebrews 13:5-6; Deuteronomy 31:6-8, 23
Joshua 1:5-9; Psalm 27:1; 118:6-9

1. Who can you trust with every area of your life?

2. Will God ever abandon you?

3. How can you trust that God will never leave you nor forsake you?

4. If you are someplace you know you should not be, what should you do?

5. Where is God when bad things happen to you?

6. If you acknowledge God in all your ways, what will He do?

NOTES:

WEEK 49
❖GRACE AND FAVOR❖
❧❧❧❧❧❧❧❧❧❧❧❧

❖DAY 1❖
Read 2 Corinthians 12:9; Proverbs 3:4
Romans 6:14; Hebrews 8:12; Ephesians 1:7-8

Grace is My unmerited favor and a manifestation of My power, exceeding what you could achieve or hope for by your own labor. My grace is a gift. I am grace and favor. If you have accepted Me as your Lord and Savior, you have grace and favor in you and on you.

My grace makes holy living possible. My grace is powerful and all-enabling to you. In your weaknesses, My grace is sufficient for you and powerful enough for you to overcome.

Father, I declare Your grace and favor is in me and is sufficient for me in my weaknesses. It is a manifestation of Your power that You give me access to in knowing You as my Lord and Savior. In Jesus' name Amen.

❖DAY 2❖
Read 2 Corinthians 12:9; Proverbs 3:4
Romans 6:14; Hebrews 8:12; Ephesians 1:7-8

If you want a long and satisfying life, never forget My Word and the things that I have taught you. Follow closely every truth that I have given you. When you do, you will have a full and rewarding life.

Hold on to My love and be faithful to all that My Word says. Let your life be shaped by integrity with My truth written upon your heart. This is how you will find favor and understanding with Me and with man (Proverbs 3:1-4 The Passion Translation).

Father, I declare I will never forget Your Word and the things that You have taught me. I will follow closely to every truth of Your Word. I will hold on to Your love and be faithful to all Your Word says. I will be shaped by integrity and put Your Word in my heart. I will find favor and understanding with You and with man. In Jesus' name Amen.

❖DAY 3❖
Read 2 Corinthians 12:9; Proverbs 3:4
Romans 6:14; Hebrews 8:12; Ephesians 1:7-8

When you accepted Me, you are no longer a slave to sin. Yes, you still may sin but you are no longer a slave to it. My power that is within you is greater than the power of any sin.

To be under law is to be trying to earn your salvation in your own strength by obeying the law, but to be under My grace is to be justified and to live by My resurrection power that dwells in you. My grace provides you all the resources to die to sin.

Father, I declare I am no longer a slave to sin and no longer under the law trying to earn salvation in my own strength by obeying the law. I am under Your grace and justified and live by Your resurrection power that dwells within me. Thank You Lord. In Jesus' name Amen.

❖DAY 4❖
Read 2 Corinthians 12:9; Proverbs 3:4
Romans 6:14; Hebrews 8:12; Ephesians 1:7-8

Grace and truth has come through Me. I am grace. I am truth. When you know My truth, My truth will set you free and deliver you. My grace and truth are the same power. I am the way, the truth, and the life. I AM.

I am the only way to the Father. My truth will prevail and teach you all that you need to know by My grace.

Father, I declare grace and truth comes through You. You are grace and truth. Your grace and truth will set me free and deliver me. You are the way, the truth, and the life. There is no other way to the Father. In Jesus' name Amen.

❖DAY 5❖
Read 2 Corinthians 12:9; Proverbs 3:4
Romans 6:14; Hebrews 8:12; Ephesians 1:7-8

I want you to believe that you are forgiven. I want you to believe that you are a person enjoying My mercy. I want you to believe that I remember your sins no more.

You are not forgiven according to what you do, but according to the riches of My grace. The New Covenant is based entirely on My unmerited favor, My grace. There is nothing for you to do, nothing for you to accomplish or perform. Only believe in Me and you will be saved by grace.

Father, I believe that I am forgiven and I am enjoying Your mercy. I know that You remember my sins no more because You took all my sins on the cross. It is nothing that I do or accomplish or perform. I only need to believe and I do believe and receive You Lord. Thank You Lord. In Jesus' name Amen.

❖DAY 6❖
Read 2 Corinthians 12:9; Proverbs 3:4
Romans 6:14; Hebrews 8:12; Ephesians 1:7-8

I want you to be righteousness conscious not sin conscious. The more you are conscious of righteousness, the more transformed you are in Me through My grace.

Stop striving to earn My righteousness. Don't do things in hopes to win points with Me like going to church or reading My Word. You cannot do anything to receive My love and acceptance. I already love and accept you. You already have My righteousness and your sins are all forgiven past, present, and future. Those who know they have been forgiven much love much. You have been forgiven much.

Father, I declare I am not sin conscious anymore but righteousness conscious. I will stop striving to do things on my own to win You over because I am loved and accepted by You. You have forgiven me of all of my sins past, present, and future. Thank You Lord. In Jesus' name Amen.

Read 2 Corinthians 12:9; Proverbs 3:4
Romans 6:14; Hebrews 8:12; Ephesians 1:7-8

1. What is grace and favor?

2. How can you have a long and satisfying life?

3. What happened when you accepted the Lord? What is being under grace mean?

4. What will set you free?

5. What does Jesus want you to believe?

6. What do you need to stop striving for?

NOTES:

WEEK 50
❖COME BOLDY INTO HIS PRESENCE❖
〜〜〜〜〜〜〜〜〜〜〜〜〜〜〜〜〜〜〜

❖DAY 1❖
Read Hebrews 4:16; Ephesians 2:18; Psalm 16:11;
Psalm 140:13; Acts 2:28; Hebrews 10:19-22

Because of My grace, you can boldly come into My presence. When you do, you will receive My mercy and grace to help you in your weaknesses.

When I walked the earth, I was tempted as you are so I can sympathize with you and help you to overcome those temptations. I did not yield to the temptations. Temptations are not sin but yielding to the temptation is sin.

Father, I declare I will boldly come into Your presence and receive mercy and grace in my weaknesses. Thank You Lord. In Jesus' name Amen.

❖DAY 2❖
Read Hebrews 4:16; Ephesians 2:18; Psalm 16:11;
Psalm 140:13; Acts 2:28; Hebrews 10:19-22

I know you do not feel worthy to come boldly into My presence but you are. Boldly means coming to My presence with no reservations, complete confidence, courage, and without fear.

I give you this boldness so come freely into My presence. I give you access through My Holy Spirit and through My shed blood on the cross.

Father, even though I may not feel worthy to come into Your presence You tell me to come boldly, without any reservations, in complete confidence, courage, and without fear into Your presence. I will freely come into Your presence. In Jesus' name Amen.

❖DAY 3❖
Read Hebrews 4:16; Ephesians 2:18; Psalm 16:11; Psalm 140:13; Acts 2:28; Hebrews 10:19-22

When you freely and boldly come into My presence, I will show you the way of life and you will receive My joy and pleasure of My presence.

I enjoy the times you come boldly into My presence and talk to Me or when you just want to draw closer to Me. I enjoy your company and want you to enjoy My company more than you do.

Father, I declare I will freely and boldly come into Your presence and when I do You will show me the way of life and I will receive Your joy and pleasure of Your presence. I enjoy Your company Lord and want to draw closer to You and know You more. In Jesus' name Amen.

❖DAY 4❖
Read Hebrews 4:16; Ephesians 2:18; Psalm 16:11; Psalm 140:13; Acts 2:28; Hebrews 10:19-22

You come to Me in prayer but you don't really enter into My presence. I still hear you and will answer your prayers, but in My presence is the fullness of joy. I give you strength when you are in My presence and when you leave My presence you can overcome any obstacle that may come your way.

You ask why you can boldly come into My presence. It is because of My shed blood on the cross which makes you righteous before Me and you lead a blameless life and do what is right in My eyes, speaking the truth. This gives you access into My presence.

Father, I declare I will enter into Your presence and receive the fullness of Your joy and receive Your strength to overcome any obstacle that may come my way. Thank You Lord. In Jesus' name Amen.

❖DAY 5❖
Read Hebrews 4:16; Ephesians 2:18; Psalm 16:11;
Psalm 140:13; Acts 2:28; Hebrews 10:19-22

Remember, I am always with you and in you. I will never leave you nor forsake you but that does not mean you are in My presence always. Coming boldly into My presence is a matter of faith and setting your mind on heavenly things rather than on earthly things.

You are not in My presence when you are doing mindless things like watching TV or reading things that are not of Me. You must come in absolute confidence in My power, wisdom, and goodness, and have your mind set on Me and My Word.

Father, I declare You are with me always. You will never leave me nor forsake me even when I am not seeking Your presence. I will come into Your presence with faith and have my mind set on You. In Jesus' name Amen.

❖DAY 6❖
Read Hebrews 4:16; Ephesians 2:18; Psalm 16:11;
Psalm 140:13; Acts 2:28; Hebrews 10:19-22

As you set your mind on Me and My Word and come boldly into My presence with confidence and faith, I will have love and compassion for you. I will protect you and shelter you from harm. My grace and mercy is for you in your times of weakness.

Be still before Me and worship Me and during these times you will enter into My presence. You have nothing to feel guilty or unworthy about if you have accepted Me, you are free to enter into My presence and enjoy My company. I look forward to our time together. Come boldly and freely into My presence.

Father, I declare I set my mind on You and Your Word and come boldly into Your presence and receive Your love, joy, mercy, and grace. I will be still before You and I worship You and enter into Your presence. I look forward to spending time in Your presence Lord. In Jesus' name Amen.

❖DAY 6-SUMMARY QUESTIONS❖
Read Hebrews 4:16; Ephesians 2:18; Psalm 16:11;
Psalm 140:13; Acts 2:28; Hebrews 10:19-22

1. Why can you boldly come into His presence?

2. What does boldness to enter His presence mean?

3. What will you receive when you freely and boldly enter into His presence?

4. What makes you righteous before Him and able to enter into His presence?

5. What does it take to enter into His presence?

6. What do I need to do to help enter into His presence?

NOTES:

WEEK 51
❖ETERNAL LIFE❖
❧❧❧❧❧❧❧❧❧❧❧

❖DAY 1❖
Read John 3:14-16; 6:47; Romans 6:23
John 14:1-3; 1 John 5:11-13, 20; John 17:1-5

Father God loved you so very much He sent Me as a gift to you, to die on the cross. If you believe in Me, you will never perish but have eternal life. Eternal life is not just an endless age, but it is the quality of life in Me.

Eternal life is now in you when you believe and accept Me as your Lord and Savior because I am eternal life. When you unite your heart to Me and believe, you experience eternal life.

Father, I declare You loved me so much You sent Jesus as a gift to me that I might be forgiven of my sins and have eternal life. Thank You for sending Jesus to die for me. In Jesus' name Amen.

❖DAY 2❖
Read John 3:14-16; 6:47; Romans 6:23
John 14:1-3; 1 John 5:11-13, 20; John 17:1-5

The wages of sin is death but Father God sent Me and gave you eternal life through your union with Me, your Lord and Savior.

Father God sent Me but I freely and gladly came to die for you. I love you as much as Father God loves you. Father God and I are one. No one took My life; I freely gave it up for you. If you have not accepted Me as Your Lord and Savior, do so for the wages of your sin is death.

Father, I declare that I have asked for Your forgiveness of my sins and have accepted You as my Lord and Savior and I will not perish but I have eternal life. In Jesus' name Amen.

❖DAY 3❖
Read John 3:14-16; 6:47; Romans 6:23
John 14:1-3; 1 John 5:11-13, 20; John 17:1-5

I have prepared a place for you and when everything is ready; I will come back for you and get you. You will then be with Me where I am. There is more than enough room for everyone who accepts Me as their Lord and Savior.

Only our Father God knows when that time will be. I am ready to return but we want none to perish. As My representative continue to evangelize and tell those around you about My love and that they can have eternal life with Father God and I and with all their family and friends who believe in Me that have gone before them. I love you and I love those that are lost. There are too many out there that do not know Me and not enough laborers to bring them in.

Father, Thank You for preparing a place for me and that when You come back for me, I will be where you are and also I will be with my family and friends that have gone before me. I will go forth and evangelize, telling others about Your love and eternal life. In Jesus' name Amen.

❖DAY 4❖
Read John 3:14-16; 6:47; Romans 6:23
John 14:1-3; 1 John 5:11-13, 20; John 17:1-5

I give you eternal life not just physical life but spiritual life. This life is only in and through accepting Me as Your Lord and Savior. Whoever has Me has life.

Whoever does not have Me, does not have life. You may think life is good for you because you are healthy and prosperous but if you do not have Me, none of those things matter because you do not have life. You will die in your sins and go to hell if you do not accept Me as your Lord and Savior. I do not want you to die in your sins. I want you to believe in Me, be forgiven of your sins and have eternal life.

Thank You, Father, for eternal life that Jesus provides because I have accepted Him as my Lord and Savior. My sins are forgiven and I have eternal life. In Jesus' name Amen.

❖DAY 5❖
Read John 3:14-16; 6:47; Romans 6:23
John 14:1-3; 1 John 5:11-13, 20; John 17:1-5

My purpose on this earth was to glorify Father God which was to make Him known which I have done. Father God and I are one and I want you to be one with Me. Father God has put everything into My hands.

Since you have accepted Me as your Lord and Savior, I have given you eternal life which is to know Father God as I know Him. I have revealed Him to you and He has given to you eternal life and all good things for life and godliness.

Father, I declare that I am one with You and I want to glorify You in my life. I have eternal life which is to know You. Jesus has revealed You to me and You have given me eternal life and all good things for life and godliness. In Jesus' name Amen.

❖DAY 6❖
Read John 3:14-16; 6:47; Romans 6:23
John 14:1-3; 1 John 5:11-13, 20; John 17:1-5

You must live in My light and obey My Word and you will experience eternal life. If you disobey My Word and walk in darkness, you are not of Me.

The love of this world and the love of our Father God are incompatible. The things of the world such as gratification of your flesh, the allurement of the things of the world, and the obsession with status and importance do not come from Me. Those who do My will, have eternal life (1 John 2:16-17).

Father, I declare I live in Your light and obey Your Word. I will experience eternal life. I will not love the world or the things of the world. I will do Your will and have eternal life. In Jesus' name Amen.

211

Read John 3:14-16; 6:47; Romans 6:23
John 14:1-3; 1 John 5:11-13, 20; John 17:1-5

1.   What is eternal life?

2.   We have eternal life through what?

3.   What has Jesus prepared for you?

4.   Eternal life is only through what?

5.   What was Jesus' purpose on the earth?

6.   What must you do to experience eternal life?

NOTES:

WEEK 52
❖ALL HIS PROMISES ARE "YES AND AMEN"❖
❧❧❧❧❧❧❧❧❧❧❧❧❧❧❧❧❧❧❧❧❧❧❧

❖DAY 1❖
Read 2 Corinthians 1:19-22; Ephesians 1:13-14
Hebrews 6:12; 2 Peter 1:3-11

All My promises and what you have and who you are in Me are a resounding "Yes and Amen" which means affirmed and confirmed.

Through Me, your "Amen" ascends to Father God for his glory. I am faithful and consistent to do what I say.

Father, I declare all Your promises are "Yes and Amen". You are faithful and consistent to do what You say. In Jesus' name Amen.

❖DAY 2❖
Read 2 Corinthians 1:19-22; Ephesians 1:13-14
Hebrews 6:12; 2 Peter 1:3-11

I have enabled you to stand firm for Me. I have commissioned you and I have identified you as My own by placing Holy Spirit in your heart as the first installment that guarantees everything I have promised you and given the inheritance to you that was promised.

I will perfect what I have begun in you through the Holy Spirit which gives Father God praise and glory.

Father, I declare You enabled me to stand firm for Christ and You have commissioned me and identified me as Your own placing the Holy Spirit in my heart as the first installment that guarantees everything You have promised me. You will perfect what You have begun in me through the Holy Spirit. In Jesus' name Amen.

Read 2 Corinthians 1:19-22; Ephesians 1:13-14
Hebrews 6:12; 2 Peter 1:3-11

My Holy Spirit given to you is the ultimate promise because without Him, you will not receive your inheritance through Me because Holy Spirit makes it possible.

As you minister to others, I will work through you confirming what you say by many miraculous signs.

Father, I declare the Holy Spirit is the ultimate promise given to me because without Him I would not receive my inheritance through Christ because Holy Spirit makes it possible. You will confirm what I say about You by many miraculous signs. In Jesus' name Amen.

❖DAY 4❖
Read 2 Corinthians 1:19-22; Ephesians 1:13-14
Hebrews 6:12; 2 Peter 1:3-11

All the promises in My Word are not necessarily automatic. You will receive the promises through faith and patience and knowing what the promises are. You need to know who you are and what you have in Me. The promises mentioned these 52 weeks are all available to you but it is your responsibility to access them.

There are many more promises in My Word not mentioned in this book. Continue to read and meditate on My Word to find all these promises and walk in them through faith and patience and you will be blessed and victorious.

Father, I declare I must believe and receive all Your promises and walk in them by faith and patience. I will continue to read and meditate on Your Word to find all the promises You have given to me. I will be blessed and victorious. In Jesus' name Amen.

Read 2 Corinthians 1:19-22; Ephesians 1:13-14
Hebrews 6:12; 2 Peter 1:3-11

By My divine power, I have given you everything you need for living a godly life. You have received all this by coming to know Me. It is because of My glory and excellence that you have been given great and precious promises.

These promises enable you to share in My divine nature and able to escape the world's corruption caused by human desires. You are to make every effort to respond to My promises. They are available to you.

Father, I declare that by Your divine power You have given me everything I need for living a godly life. I receive these promises by knowing You. It is because of Your glory and excellence that I have been given great and precious promises. They enable me to share in Your divine nature and escape the world's corruptions. Thank You Lord. In Jesus' name Amen.

Read 2 Corinthians 1:19-22; Ephesians 1:13-14
Hebrews 6:12; 2 Peter 1:3-11

In view of all this, you need to supplement your faith with these things listed: moral excellence, moral excellence with knowledge, knowledge with self-control, self-control with patient endurance, patient endurance with godliness, godliness with brotherly affection, and brotherly affection with love for everyone.

The more you grow in these, the more productive and useful you will be in the knowledge of Me. Do these things and you will never fall away and you will receive My promises.

Father, I will supplement my faith with moral excellence, knowledge, self-control, patient endurance, godliness, brotherly affection, and love for everyone. The more I grow in these, the more productive and useful I will be in knowing You. I receive everything I need for godly living by knowing You more. In Jesus' name Amen.

Read 2 Corinthians 1:19-22; Ephesians 1:13-14
Hebrews 6:12; 2 Peter 1:3-11

1. God's promises and who you are and what you have in Christ are what?

2. What has God enabled you to do and what has He identified you as? What will He perfect in you?

3. What is the ultimate promise given to you?

4. What will you receive God's promises through?

5. By His divine power, what has He given to you? What do they enable you to do?

6. What do we need to grow in to be more productive and useful in the knowledge of Jesus?

NOTES:

Prayer for Salvation and Baptism of the Holy Spirit

Heavenly Father, I come to You in the name of Jesus. I know that I am a sinner and have been separated from You. Your Word says whosoever shall call upon the name of the Lord [invoking, adoring, and worshiping the Lord Christ] shall be saved (Acts 2:21 Amplified Bible, Classic Edition). I am calling on You. I pray and ask Jesus to come into my heart and be Lord of my life. I confess that Jesus is Lord, and I believe in my heart that God raised Him from the dead. I repent of sin. I renounce it. I renounce the devil and everything he stands for. Jesus is my Lord.

I am now reborn! I am a Christian—a child of Almighty God! I am also asking You to fill me with the Holy Spirit. Holy Spirit, rise up within me as I praise God. I fully expect to speak with other tongues as You give me the utterance (Acts 2:4). In Jesus' name Amen.

Begin to praise God for filling you with the Holy Spirit. Speak those words and syllables you receive, not in your own language, but the language given to you by the Holy Spirit. You have to use your own voice. God will not force you to speak. Get into a Spirit-filled church and stay in the Word of God.

Made in the USA
Monee, IL
14 November 2020